EASY PORTUGUESE
COOKBOOK

Easy
PORTUGUESE
Cookbook

Recipes to Bring Home the Flavors of Portugal

Stacy Silva-Boutwell
Photography by Iain Bagwell

ROCKRIDGE
PRESS

To my mother and father for giving me the strength and abilities I have today, my husband for lovingly being by my side, and my children, Lucas and Alaina, for whom I do everything.

For general information on our other products and services or to obtain technical support, please contact our Customer Care Department within the United States at (866) 744-2665, or outside the United States at (510) 253-0500.

Rockridge Press publishes its books in a variety of electronic and print formats. Some content that appears in print may not be available in electronic books, and vice versa.

TRADEMARKS: Rockridge Press and the Rockridge Press logo are trademarks or registered trademarks of Callisto Media Inc. and/or its affiliates, in the United States and other countries, and may not be used without written permission. All other trademarks are the property of their respective owners. Rockridge Press is not associated with any product or vendor mentioned in this book.

Interior and Cover Designer: Mando Daniel

Art Producer: Karen Williams

Editor: Justin Hartung

Production Manager: Martin Worthington

Production Editor: Melissa Edeburn

Author photo courtesy of Alexandria Mauck Photography.

Photography © 2020 Iain Bagwell. Food styling by Katelyn Hardwick.

Cover (clockwise): Roasted Chouriço and Potatoes (page 37), Custard Tart Cups (page 92), Piri Piri Chicken (page 83); Back Cover: White Peach Sangria (page 105).

ISBN: Print 978-1-64611-644-7 | eBook 978-1-64611-645-4

R0

Contents

Introduction
Bom dia!

"There is an egg on my steak," my non-Portuguese (soon-to-be) husband said on our first date at a restaurant in Fall River, Massachusetts. "Of course," I calmly replied. Later, he recounted this story at our wedding, and the guests chuckled. I grew up in a Portuguese neighborhood, so I sometimes forget this kind of food isn't the norm for everybody, but it is for me and most of the people who live around me. São Miguel, where my parents were born, is the largest of the nine Azorean islands off the coast of Portugal.

Just as my grandmother showed her, my mother taught me how to get the egg on that steak to look and taste just right. I learned to spoon hot oil over the egg instead of frying it on both sides. And I learned to marinate the steak before frying it in beer, garlic, and pepper.

In my lifetime, I have seen São Miguel transform, as most of Portugal has. When I was 11 years old, my grandmother, Vavó Olinda, took me on a trip to her village, Povoação. At that time, moving about the island required us to drive treacherous mountain roads with no guardrails. There were only two telephones for the whole village, and my great-aunt, Titia Belmira, had a bathroom built into an outdoor structure, much like an outhouse.

Today, the infrastructure has been vastly improved, with a modern highway stretching across the island. Plumbing and communication have been modernized. The mineral-rich hot springs that were used to cook *cozido*—a traditional boiled dinner heated by the steam from those springs—are now just as famous for their use as medicinal spa baths. The black-sand beaches where I would find *lapas* (limpets) are now dotted with tourists who are drawn to the photogenic volcanic ash. And the beautifully landscaped countryside covered in blue hydrangeas where I have enjoyed many picnics over the years now lures hikers and adventure enthusiasts from countries near and far. Portugal has been discovered.

On my blog, *The Portuguese American Mom* (thePAMom.com), I share my decades-long experience with Portuguese food with the goal of helping readers re-create my family's favorite recipes and discover dishes from some of the country's culinary hot spots. This book collects some of those recipes and also offers plenty of new mouthwatering and updated options, all of which you'll be able to make with ingredients you can find at your local market.

Back to *Bife à Portuguesa*, that egg-topped steak dish that freaked out my husband. When I make it, I use the *pimenta moida* that my father grinds from fresh chile peppers each harvest and preserves in jars. You see, Portuguese food is a family affair—in preparation, cooking, and dining.

CHAPTER ONE

Portuguese Cooking 101

Portuguese cuisine is a celebration of simplicity. It doesn't involve a lot of complicated techniques. If you work with fresh, high-quality, organic, and unprocessed ingredients, half the work is done for you. This chapter describes some of the fundamentals. With a few basic marinades and sauces, you can transform almost any protein into a main dish. Pair that protein with rice and potatoes, and you've created a meal found in almost any family-style Portuguese restaurant. For example, Pan Fried "Pork Chomps" (page 74), prepared in a marinade of Pimenta Moida (page 121) and fresh garlic and accompanied by rice and fried potatoes, is similar yet completely different from Portuguese Steak (page 80).

A True Melting Pot

Long before the United States became the world's largest melting pot, Portuguese exploration and expansion resulted in a kingdom that epitomized the term. The Azorean Islands, lovingly referred to as "As Ilhas," were an important stopping point for traders and sailors traveling to and from Lisbon, aptly nicknamed "Immigrant City." Portugal has been absorbing new people, ideas, and foods from around the globe for centuries. Just recently, the prime minister, Antonio Costa, called for an increase of 75,000 new immigrants annually in an effort to stabilize the economy. This spirit goes both ways, as Portuguese migrants are found on every inhabited continent. But no matter where the Portuguese go, generations upon generations still consider Portugal home, and when they come back, they bring with them culinary influences that contribute to the ever-evolving flavors of Portugal.

History

Prince Henry the Navigator is by far the most recognizable and formative figure in Portuguese history. His contributions to the science of sailing are legendary the world over. He founded a school that fostered the development of a system of navigation in a time when it was still readily accepted that the world was flat. In the late 14th century, the spice trade was largely controlled by Arab traders. Prince Henry sponsored expeditions that brought about the Age of Discovery. Later, in the 15th century, not long after the prince died, Vasco de Gama sailed around the Cape of Good Hope and established a route connecting Europe to India by sea.

With exploration comes discovery. Prince Henry wanted to grow the Portuguese Empire, and he hoped to spread Portuguese influence around the world. A driving force of colonization, Prince Henry led Portugal in establishing colonies in Asia, Africa, and South America. The prince advised his sailors to bring new plants and seeds back to Portugal from its colonies. In the centuries that followed, Portuguese sailors introduced pineapple and tea from Brazil to the Azores. They also transported coffee from Africa to South America, where it is now an economic cornerstone. Citrus trees full of lemons and oranges were planted in the Algarve. Olives and figs, which are now found throughout Portugal, were transplanted from various parts of the world. Intensely flavored vegetables and spices, like peppers from Africa and cinnamon from India, forever changed Portuguese flavor. More than half of all Portuguese desserts involve cinnamon, as do some meat dishes, and peppers are indispensable. These many influences are essential facets of Portuguese cuisine to this day.

The Culinary Scene Today

For many years, the Portuguese culinary scene was considered rustic and largely focused on foods that could feed a family with minimal cost. Those roots are still evident today as old recipes have become trusted family comfort foods. Meals like Holy Ghost Soup (page 54) were meant to feed an entire village, and *papas*, a warm breakfast porridge made of little more than milk, fed families going through tough economic times. Only on holidays or during celebrations would people feast on a whole roast or a casserole of *bacalhau* (salt cod). But now, in better economic times, the restaurant scene in Portugal has elevated special-occasion foods and incorporated even more international influence. Foods like Skewered Beef (page 81), normally reserved for Christmas or a church feast, are now commonly found favorites at Portuguese restaurants everywhere.

Regional Cheat Sheet

Portuguese cuisine is generally focused on locally sourced ingredients. Fortunately, this philosophy fits in well with the farm-to-table food trend that's happening around the world. From Costa Verde, known as the Green Coast in the north—famous for Green Soup (page 52), a pureed potato soup made with kale and *chouriço*—to the Algarve in the south, known for its seafood and fig groves, the regions of Portugal make the most of the ingredients that grow there.

Costa Verde (Green Coast)

What to Know: The northernmost point of Portugal, Costa Verde is green and lush.

What It's Known For: Although not located in Portugal's wine country, two of the country's most popular wines, Porto and Vinho Verde, are produced in this region.

Iconic Dish: Green Soup (page 52), a simple soup made with pureed potatoes, kale, and thinly sliced chouriço, is served throughout the country and in just about every Portuguese restaurant around the world.

Costa de Prata (Silver Coast)

What to Know: Situated just north of Lisbon and stretching nearly to Spain, this large section of Portugal is known for its picturesque architecture and beautiful beaches.

What It's Known For: As a large area of this region falls along the Atlantic Ocean, seafood is abundant, but baked goods are also a highlight here.

Iconic Dish: Vavó's Sponge Cake (page 95), is based on a popular Portuguese sponge cake, originated on the Silver Coast, as did the delightfully dry popovers covered in a royal icing, called Popovers with Lemon Icing (page 94).

Montanhas (Mountains)

What to Know: This is the only region in all of Portugal that does not have even a small portion bordering some part of the ocean. A mountainous region bordering Spain, Montanhas is known mainly for its Douro wine area.

What It's Known For: Goat and chicken are center stage in this region, as are sausages made from various livestock and even the flavorful *morcela* (blood sausage).

Iconic Dish: *Tortas* are meal-size sandwiches made of leftovers fried into an egg omelet and are a popular dish in this region.

Lisbon Area

What to Know: The Portuguese capital, Lisbon, and its surrounding suburbs make up this region, which has a mild climate because it lies in the warmer southern half of the country's west coast.

What It's Known For: *Fado*, a deeply soulful melancholy music heard in many Portuguese restaurants, originated in Lisbon. As a seaside metropolis, Lisbon is known for its legendary port wine and diversity of seafood, which, along with cheese, are among the most popular foods of the region.

Iconic Dish: Little Necks in Garlic Wine Sauce (page 24) is a simple dish that is almost as much about dunking fire-grilled bread into the savory broth as the delicious clams it showcases.

Alentejo

What to Know: Just a short 1½-hour drive west of Lisbon, spanning down to the Algarve region, Alentejo covers almost a third of Portugal's land mass. It is one of the few areas of Portugal that is known for agriculture and livestock, rather than seafood.

What It's Known For: Known as the "Wine Region of Portugal," this area is popular with tourists for its vineyards. But it also boasts some of the best olive groves in the country, as well as superior cured meats such as *presunto*, a cured ham made from Alentejo black pigs.

Iconic Dish: Found in almost any Portuguese restaurant, Alentejo-Style Roasted Cubed Pork with Little Necks (page 72) is made with marinated cubed pork, fried potatoes, and little neck clams, all in a delectable *molho* (sauce).

Algarve

What to Know: At the southernmost point of the country, Algarve is situated on the Atlantic Ocean and is one of the last stops before entering the Mediterranean Sea. This region is one of the trendiest vacation spots in the country.

What It's Known For: Figs are among the region's most beloved fruits, but some of the world's highest-quality cork is grown here (and in the bordering southern part of Alentejo) and imported all over the world.

Iconic Dish: Aside from its abundant seafood dishes, Algarve is known for its Petiscos de Taberna (page 17). These plates of small bites can be enjoyed throughout the region with some local *cerveja* (beer).

Madeira

What to Know: Considered the Hawaii of Portugal, this island in the Atlantic Ocean is closer to the coast of Africa than to Portugal and a significant distance away from the Azores. Madeira is a mountainous island boasting an abundance of exotic vegetation because of its high elevations.

What It's Known For: World-renowned Madeira wine is by far the most significant thing to come from this region, but Madeira is also known for its small sweet bananas, bay leaves, and rare tropical fruits.

Iconic Dish: Skewered Beef (page 81) is salted meat rubbed with spices, skewered, and cooked over an open flame until charred and delicious. You will find this dish at feasts all over Portugal.

Azores

What to Know: The Azorean Islands are a group of nine islands located in the Atlantic Ocean. They have a climate that's usually a little milder than Boston, which is just a 5-hour flight away from the main island of St. Michael.

What It's Known For: Azores is known for its bountiful agriculture and dairy. Cheese, tea, and tropical fruit such as pineapples, passion fruit, and bananas are abundant. Much of the islands' population is also highly skilled at fishing.

Iconic Dishes: Holy Ghost Soup (page 54) is eaten to celebrate the regional feast of the Holy Ghost. Equally notable is Cozido, a boiled dinner of meats, sausages, and root vegetables that's traditionally lowered into the ground and cooked by natural hot water springs. You'll find a recipe for a stovetop version on page 76.

The 5 Foundations of Portuguese Cuisine

Three main factors greatly affect Portugal's cuisine: its natural geographic locale, colonial history, and economy. The foundational ingredients are a direct result of one or more of these factors. Portugal's vast coastline and great many volcanic islands led to the prominent placement of seafood in the country's cuisine. Moreover, its cuisine is influenced by flavors from all over the world as a result of the expansion of the Portuguese Empire by Prince Henry the Navigator. Portugal was once the most powerful country in the world, but following its colonial wars, the economy had a major downturn that lasted centuries, forcing Portuguese homemakers to get creative as they stretched the family food resources.

Seafood

A staple in nearly every region of Portugal, seafood is by far the most versatile foods in the country. Bacalhau is the national food of this seafaring people, as Portuguese fishermen would travel far into the cold waters of the north Atlantic and salt the cod right on board, preserving it for the months-long journey back to port. This beloved fish is prepared throughout the country in as many ways as there are days in the year. Along with bacalhau, many other varieties of seafood are popular: shellfish (including clams and limpets known as *lapas*), sardines that are grilled or pan-fried whole, fried horse mackerel with *molho* (sauce), and prized octopus that's stewed or roasted. If there is any one protein the Portuguese people know how to cook and depend on, it's seafood.

Pork

You can tell a lot about a person by how they tend to their pig—or so the Portuguese saying goes. A well-tended and clean pigpen is a matter of pride in a Portuguese family's *quintal*, or back garden. When I visited Portugal as a child, I observed how my cousins would hose down their family pig's cement pen several times a day. A pig acts as a garbage disposal of sorts, eating any leftover vegetation, and also serves as a major food source for the year.

As the main livestock protein in Portugal, pork is used in a variety of sausages, in the boiled dinner known as *cozido*, in pan-fried chops, and in the delectable marinated *caçoila*. Just about every part of the pig is rendered useful in Portuguese cooking. Even the fat is melted down and made into lard, which is traditionally how salted meat was stored throughout the year. The slaughter of a pig is almost ritualistic in a gathering called a *matança*.

When I was about 5 years old, my family bought a very large hog. The whole family gathered in our backyard to slaughter and divide up the animal. Its blood was drained to make fresh blood sausage known as *morcela*. Sections of the meat were butchered and carefully wrapped in white butcher's paper. And, finally, the intestines were emptied, cleaned, and filled with seasoned meat and bits of fat, which were then smoked to make *chouriço*.

Beans, Rice, and Potatoes

Starchy legumes, grains, and root vegetables make up most of the sides you'll encounter in Portuguese cooking. All three are a major component of most soups and stews, and often serve as a low-cost meal filler. Chicken and rice is a staple in almost every country, and the Portuguese preparation, a combination of onions, potatoes, and a gentle hint of tomato in the background, is simply mouthwatering. Beans are often baked in dishes, like Baked Beans (page 34) or added to soups and stews like Meat and Bean Stew (page 48). Potatoes can be fried, roasted, or boiled in equal measure throughout Portuguese cuisine and are often as much a part of the dish as the protein it is supporting.

Soup

A staple in any Portuguese home, soup is known not only as a starter to a meal but also a main dish when served with bread. Sunday is often thought of as soup day, and the soup that is lovingly made after church can be stretched to feed an entire family for the whole week if need be. In tough economic times, to which Portugal has been no stranger, soup has provided the average Portuguese family with healthy well-balanced sustenance and comfort. Portuguese kale (closer to collard greens than American curly kale) was a featured ingredient in Portuguese soup long before it became a trendy health food. Among the most commonly enjoyed soups are Kale Soup (page 44), Green Soup (page 52), and Bean Soup (page 53), which are often called *sopa de feijão* and *caldeirada*.

Spices

Flavor is rich and abundant in Portuguese cuisine thanks to Prince Henry the Navigator and Vasco de Gama, who worked to secure the first route from Europe to Asia by sea. As a direct result, spices like paprika, cinnamon, curry, and many types of peppers are present in Portuguese cooking today. One of the most indispensable uses of peppers is in a wet spice known as *pimenta moida*.

PIMENTA MOIDA

It's September in New England, and farmers' markets are bustling, but we wait until the full moon to go to the one in our nearby city. According to my late grandfather, Vavô Fernando (a master gardener), we should wait until the peppers are picked the day after the full moon. This ensures we'll get the best bushel for grinding into our family's most used spice, pimenta moida.

Pimenta Moida (page 121) is a cornerstone of Portuguese cooking. Spicy chiles grown under the hot summer sun all season long are ripened to their red fullness and available only a few short weeks a year. We get to the market, gather our bushel (after searching down the best price from the many vendors), and take them home to be processed by hand. This is my father's task every year. Each family has a different way of processing their chiles, depending on the level of heat desired in their cooking. My father cuts the peppers lengthwise and removes all the seeds he possibly can, cuts off the stems, and attaches the old-fashioned hand-crank grinder to an outdoor table. My mother places a very large steel bowl underneath to catch the freshly ground pepper, which is transferred to a large pot, salted, and covered with a lid.

Over the next few days, the peppers undergo a "boiling" process, which doesn't actually involve an external heat source; instead, the salt reacts to the heat of the pepper. Much of the pepper's heat is released through this process. Once the "boiling" comes to an end, it's time to add a bit of preservative and store the peppers in jars for our year's supply.

PIRI PIRI

Portuguese cooking isn't known for being spicy. Pepper is mainly used as a flavor component rather than a source of heat, and many Portuguese cooks take care to remove spicy seeds from any chiles they use. When a recipe is spicy, however, you have piri piri to thank. The Swahili name of this fiery sauce translates to "pepper pepper." The former Portuguese colonies of Angola and Mozambique both lay claim to its origin, but no one has been able to pin down which is correct. After the revolutionary wars of independence fought by these countries, Portuguese soldiers brought piri piri home with them. The sauce is usually made with very hot chiles, red wine vinegar, garlic, and paprika. Piri Piri Chicken (page 83) and Shrimp Mozambique (page 60) are popular dishes that showcase this fiery sauce.

Wines of Portugal

Wine is an important part of everyday life throughout Portugal. Although the country is listed as number 84 on the world population list, it is the eleventh largest producer of wine in the world, with more than 22 million acres of land dedicated to its production. In recent decades, the wine region in Alentejo has become increasingly recognized for its distinctive vineyards and innovative wine-processing centers. But long before Alentejo became a trendy tourist destination, other areas of the country were producing world-famous Port, Vinho Verde, and Madeira. Additionally, Portuguese people do not leave the wine-making to the professionals. Just about every family has at least one member who makes their own wine, usually in the basement from grapes grown in their garden. My family treasures my late Vavó Silva's old wooden wine press.

Red Wine

Robust, full-bodied, and deeply flavorful, red wine from the Douro region pairs especially well with hearty, meaty roasts, steaks, and stews. In general, a dry red from Douro is like a very deep cabernet. Alicante Bouschet, also from Douro, is a sweet red with notes of blackberries, blueberries, and maple syrup. This wine is best reserved for an after-dinner treat. Moving on to the Dão area, Jaen, or Mencía, is a beautifully smooth dry red that has berry notes of its own but is also earthy and flavorful. Red wine is a main ingredient in many stews (and enjoyed by the chef as they cook).

White Wine

Vinho Verde is by far the most well-known Portuguese white wine. It's modestly priced and served in Portuguese restaurants near and far. Its name, meaning "green wine," refers not to its color but rather its young age—it's released a mere three to six months after harvest, which makes it a bit fizzy. This dry, refreshing wine pairs well with seafood such as grilled sardines. Arinto is a wine to look out for if you seek a well-aged (and slightly pricier) pick. This wine is slightly bitter and quite acidic, and makes a lovely pairing for grilled fish or Taro Root with Onion Medley (page 33). Another popular white wine, sparkling espumante, is often enjoyed during celebrations and produced in regions throughout the country. It can also add a bit of pizzazz to White Peach Sangria (page 105).

Madeira

The story of Madeira wine goes something like this. Madeira was an essential stop along the trade route around Africa to Asia. Portuguese sailors stopped to fill up on freshly made wine, which they stored on the ship. The wine was battered about and sat in the hot sun on the ship's difficult journey back to the mainland. The sailors were advised to dispose of the wine, but they drank it anyway and realized there was something special about it. One thing led to another, and this throwaway wine became trendy and sought after by wealthy citizens. Madeira continues to be a popular party wine, although it can be served with a meal as well.

Port

Port is by far the oldest and most famous wine of Portugal. It's traditionally a fortified sweet red wine made from combining a variety of different grapes grown in the Douro area, where Porto is located. In recent years, the Douro region has expanded port wine to include white and rose varieties. Port wine is most often paired with a good Portuguese cheese, as it balances the sharpness with its thick sweetness, and is most commonly enjoyed before or after a meal.

Other Drinks

Sangria, a festive mix of wine, fruit, and liquor, dates back to the Age of Discovery, when tropical fruits were making their way to Portugal from South America and the Caribbean. Both Portuguese and Spanish sailors took a liking to this easy-to-drink sweet concoction. Popular varieties include classic Red Sangria (page 104) and White Peach Sangria (page 105), the latter of which is often served with *petiscos* (bar snacks).

Portuguese gin, an artisanal specialty in the northern region of the country, and cachaça, fermented sugarcane juice, are popular liquors for mixing cocktails throughout the country. Liqueurs play an equally big role in Portuguese cocktails: Licor Beirão is aromatic and spicy with a soft sweetness, while anisette offers a potent licorice punch. Cocktails made from these libations include the refreshing and trendy Caipirão (page 110) and Cherry Anisette Cocktail (page 108). I've updated some favorites, too, like Stacy's Tropical Poncha (page 109), my tropical twist on the popular Madeiran cocktail, and the show-stopping Queimada (page 112), a drink you literally light on fire!

Don't Call Them Tapas: Petiscos

The Portuguese snacks called petiscos are much less formal than their cousin, Spanish tapas. Simple olives, stored cheeses, pickled lupini beans, and, of course, the country's famous bacalhau are enjoyed at bars around the country. It is routine to stop by a tavern on the way home from work for a glass of wine and a small plate of petiscos enjoyed with friends. Dinners are often served after 8 p.m., so the little tide-me-over treat is a natural way of life.

At Christmastime, nuts and dried fruits are added to the mix, and most Portuguese households will have them on hand for unannounced visitors. (The ability to entertain at the drop of a hat is a key component of Portugal's culinary culture.) If you are thinking about adding something a little different to your cocktail party, petiscos are a great way to dive into Portuguese cooking.

About the Recipes

As you make your way through these recipes, be sure to read the tips and tricks, which include pairing suggestions and more. Use fresh ingredients whenever they are available. I've included substitutions for ingredients not often found at your local grocer in many of the recipes and in the following chart under Easy Substitutions. Also, feel free to experiment. Once you have the basics down, you can adjust to suit your family's palate.

Most important, whether you are re-creating a trip to this part of the Iberian peninsula or just taking a virtual culinary tour through Portugal, have fun! Portuguese food is rooted in the history of the whole world and has influences from parts far and wide. This cuisine should be celebrated and enjoyed with friends and family, as it has been for centuries.

Easy Substitutions

While the recipes in this book provide tips for easy substitutions whenever possible, a few ingredients are frequently used, so it's a good idea to see if you can find them at your local grocery store before you start cooking. I've also provided online resources at the end of this book. If you can't find these ingredients, here are some widely available substitutions.

Ingredient	Where to use it	Substitution
Chouriço: A smoked pork sausage flavored with paprika, garlic, wine, vinegar, and white pepper	Soups, stews, and as an accompaniment to roasts or just on its own	Pork soaked in Chouriço Marinade (page 116) and seared to seal in the flavor; linguiça; or smoked Spanish chorizo
Pimenta moida (page 121): Ground red chile that has been preserved using salt and a "boiling" process that draws heat from the chiles' own capsaicin (see a tutorial for making pimenta moida on my website, thePAMom.com)	Soups, stews, roasts, sauces, toppings, and stuffing—almost everything	Thai chili paste—just remember to reduce the amount, as it's much hotter than pimenta moida
Portuguese All Spice (page 123): A blend made from paprika, garlic, pepper, and other spices	Mostly in sauces and saucy food	Sweet paprika

4 Menus to Try

Once you get familiar with the recipes in this book, what better way to share what you've learned than by throwing a Portuguese-themed evening? Here are some suggestions for a festive gathering, a traditional family dinner, and even a romantic date night.

Cocktail Party

Red Sangria (page 104) or White Peach Sangria (page 105)

Caipirão (page 110)

Wines: Madeira, Arinto, and Port

Cheese: São Jorge, Serra de Estrella, and Azeitão

Codfish Cakes (page 22)

Chouriço and Peppers Finger Sandwiches (page 26)

Pepper-Stuffed Potatoes (page 21)

Coconut Custard Tarts (page 91)

Date Night

Green Soup (page 52)

Skewered Beef (page 81)

Tomato Rice (page 30)

Fried Whole Potatoes (page 31)

Glass of Madeira wine

Flan Pudding with Caramel Sauce (page 88)

Queimada (page 112)

Family Dinner

Chicken and Rice (page 82)

Bread Rolls (page 127)

Wine Cooler (page 106)

Biscuit Rings (page 96) with tea

Dinner Party

Firefighter Chouriço (page 25)

Bean Soup (page 53)

Portuguese Steak (page 80)

Fried Whole Potatoes (page 31)

White rice

Fried Cinnamon Sugar Toast (page 97) with espresso

CHAPTER TWO

Petiscos

Enjoying these small bites is a regular part of life in Portugal. People often stop at cafés or taverns for a snack on the way home from work, and there are now even trendy *petisqueiras* with menus dedicated to petiscos. Kick off your next dinner or cocktail party with a few of the recipes in this chapter, or just enjoy them as a snack at home whenever a craving strikes.

Little Necks in Garlic Wine Sauce (page 24)

Boiled Chestnuts

CASTANHAS COZIDAS

Prep time: 1 minute | Cook time: 45 minutes

Portuguese grocers the world over start carrying chestnuts in late October, not for roasting (as is typical in the United States), but for boiling. Enjoyed after a holiday meal long after dessert and coffee (at least in my family), these chestnuts are creamy and sweet. **SERVES 4 TO 6**

2 pounds chestnuts

1. In a large stockpot, bring 6 quarts water to a boil over high heat.
2. Add the chestnuts, cover, and lower the heat to medium-low. Simmer until tender, checking the water level periodically and adding more water to ensure the pot does not dry out, about 45 minutes.
3. Serve warm or at room temperature.

HELPFUL HINT:

Be sure to set a timer while the chestnuts are cooking. I cannot tell you how many times this boiling pot has slipped my mind, with disastrous results.

WHEN IN PORTUGAL:

These chestnuts are meant to be savored and shared with friends and family from a big bowl in the center of the table. Provide small paring knives for peeling back the skin, and place another bowl on the table for collecting the peels.

Roasted Pumpkin Seeds

SEMENTES DE ABÓBORA ASSADAS

Prep time: 10 minutes | **Cook time:** 30 minutes

Around Halloween, when you're carving your pumpkins, consider putting the seeds aside for this fun family activity. Kids love getting their hands messy, but they'll love snacking on these roasted pumpkin seeds even more. Adjust the cayenne pepper to suit your family's palate. **SERVES 2 TO 4**

---

2 cups fresh pumpkin seeds from 1 medium pumpkin

1 tablespoon paprika

1 tablespoon fine kosher salt

1 tablespoon granulated garlic

1 teaspoon red pepper flakes

½ teaspoon cayenne pepper

1. Preheat the oven to 350°F. Line a baking sheet with parchment paper.

2. Remove the pumpkin seeds from the pumpkin, rinse them completely, and place them in a medium bowl. Do not dry; set aside.

3. In a resealable container, mix together the paprika, salt, granulated garlic, red pepper flakes, and cayenne pepper.

4. Add 2 to 3 tablespoons spice mixture for every 1 cup pumpkin seeds and stir to combine. (You can store any leftover spice mix in a resealable container at room temperature for up to 3 months.) Spread out the seeds in a single layer on the prepared sheet.

5. Bake for 20 minutes. Stir the seeds and bake for an additional 10 minutes. Let cool.

6. Break up any big pieces and serve.

HELPFUL HINT:

If your family likes more spice, use Hungarian paprika.

WHEN IN PORTUGAL:

These easy, tasty treats are enjoyed year-round by Portuguese people all over the world. They are commonly found in any shop carrying Portuguese goods and are served up while watching a *futebol* game or at a local pub or café.

Stuffed Eggs
OVOS RECHEADOS

Prep time: 1 hour | Cook time: 20 minutes

You can thank my Vavó Olinda for this recipe. I asked her to make it with me in her tiny kitchen so I could learn the proper technique. These eggs require a little effort, but once you eat them, you'll find the extra energy was worthwhile. **SERVES 6**

---

6 hard-boiled eggs, peeled

2 cups uncooked Thanksgiving Stuffing (page 36)

1 cup vegetable oil

2 large eggs, beaten

1. Cut the hard-boiled eggs in half, and place the yolks in a large bowl. Set aside the whites on a plate.

2. Mash the yolks with a fork. Add the stuffing, and stir to combine.

3. With wet hands, place 2 tablespoons stuffing mixture into each hard-boiled egg half, forming each into the shape of a whole egg. You should have something that is half egg white and half stuffing. Place the stuffed eggs on a plate and set aside at room temperature for at least 30 minutes. (If longer, place in the refrigerator without covering for up to 8 hours.)

4. When ready to cook, in a heavy-bottomed nonstick skillet, heat the oil over medium heat.

5. In a small bowl, beat the raw eggs.

6. Test the temperature of the oil by placing a small amount of leftover stuffing or the end of a wooden spoon into the oil. If bubbles form, the oil is ready for frying.

7. Line a large plate with paper towels.

8. Gently place each stuffed egg into the beaten egg, turning them to ensure they are completely covered, and let the excess egg drip away. Place the dipped egg into the hot oil and fry, turning the egg every 2 minutes or so with tongs, until it is golden brown. If your skillet fits 12 eggs without crowding, fry all of them at once. If not, fry them in batches of 6. Using tongs, transfer the eggs onto the lined plate.

9. Serve hot or at room temperature.

WHEN IN PORTUGAL:
You won't find this recipe on many restaurant menus, which is exactly what makes it so special.

Pepper-Stuffed Potatoes

BATATAS COM PIMENTA

Prep time: 5 to 10 minutes | **Cook time:** 25 minutes

I don't think I can remember a family celebration that didn't include a big tray of these creamy potatoes. Stuffed with a briny pepper mixture, they can be served warm or at room temperature. Pack them up for a picnic.
SERVES 4 TO 6

---

8 small to medium Red Bliss
  potatoes
½ teaspoon kosher salt

3 garlic cloves, divided
¼ cup olive oil

½ cup Pimenta Moida
  (page 121)

1. Slice into each potato about two-thirds of the way through. The potato should still be whole, only allowing a pocket in which to put the pepper stuffing. (But don't worry if your knife goes all the way through; just sandwich the pepper stuffing with the two potato halves.) Place the potatoes in a large pot and cover with 6 quarts cold water. Add the salt and stir to combine. Crush 1 garlic clove and add it to the pot. Bring to a boil over high heat, and cook until the cut in the potatoes starts to separate and they are fork tender. Turn off the heat and let the liquid cool for a few minutes. Drain the potatoes and set aside to cool.

2. Run the remaining 2 garlic cloves through a garlic press or mince them with a sharp knife. In a small skillet, pour in the olive oil and add the garlic. Sauté over medium heat for 2 minutes. Add the Pimenta Moida, lower the heat to low, and cook until hot, about 5 minutes. Let cool slightly.

3. Divide the pepper mixture evenly among the potatoes and serve warm.

EASY SUBSTITUTION:
If you don't have Pimenta Moida handy, try using Thai chili paste, but be aware that it's a bit spicier, so adjust the amount to your palate. Also, if you want to fancy this dish up a bit, consider using fingerling potatoes and serve them as an appetizer.

Codfish Cakes

BOLINHOS DE BACALHAU

Prep time: 30 minutes | **Cook time:** 20 minutes

When I was growing up, one of my favorite spots was our local Portuguese fish market, which served up a variety of large and small golden fried fish and these delightful cod cakes. In Portugal, they're found in every fish market and also in pubs and cafés. **SERVES 4 TO 6**

¾ pound dried salt cod

3 medium potatoes, peeled

1 cup canola oil, plus
 1 tablespoon, divided

½ medium onion, minced

2 teaspoons minced fresh
 flat-leaf parsley

1 large egg

Kosher salt

1. Place the salt cod in a large sauce pan and cover with cold water. Bring to a boil over high heat. Drain the water, refill with cold water, and bring to a boil again. Repeat this once more. Drain the water, mash the cod with a fork, and set aside.

2. Place the potatoes in a large pan, cover with cold water, and bring to a boil over high heat. Lower the heat to medium-low and simmer until tender, about 20 minutes. Mash the potatoes and set aside.

3. In a small skillet, heat 1 tablespoon canola oil over medium heat. Add the onion and cook until translucent, about 4 minutes. Remove from the heat and set aside.

4. Add the cod, onion, and parsley to the mashed potatoes and stir to combine. Add the egg and stir to combine.

5. Using about 2 tablespoons cod-potato mixture, use 2 spoons to form an oblong cake. Set the cake on a large plate. Repeat with the rest of the mixture.

6. Line another large plate with paper towels.

7. In a large skillet, heat 1 cup canola oil over medium-high heat. To test the temperature, dip the end of a wooden spoon into the oil. If bubbles form, the oil is ready. Carefully place the cakes into the skillet. Lower the heat to medium and fry, turning the cakes periodically, until golden brown, 10 to 15 minutes. Transfer the cakes to the lined plate. Season with salt.

8. Let cool completely and serve.

PAIR IT WITH:

These are one of the most popular snacks in Portuguese culture and are best enjoyed with a cold beer. Consider doubling or tripling the recipe the next time you invite your friends over to watch a big football game.

Little Necks in Garlic Wine Sauce

AMÊIJOAS À BULHÃO PATO

Prep time: 30 minutes | **Cook time:** 12 to 15 minutes

A perfect starter to any meal, this dish is meant to be shared with friends—a good reason to double the recipe. It's served with toasted slices of rustic bread for sopping up the broth. **SERVES 2 TO 4**

---

12 little neck clams or cherrystone clams, well-scrubbed

5 tablespoons olive oil, divided

1 small onion, halved and very thinly sliced

6 garlic cloves, crushed and coarsely chopped

1 cup dry white wine

½ teaspoon kosher or sea salt

¼ teaspoon freshly ground white pepper

¼ cup chopped fresh flat-leaf parsley

3 lemon slices, for garnish

1 loaf Portuguese Vienna bread or a French baguette, sliced

1. Soak the clams in cold salted water for 30 minutes. Change out the water and salt every 10 minutes. Each clam should be closed tight, indicating they are alive. If a clam does not close tightly, toss it.

2. Preheat the oven to 400°F.

3. In a medium skillet, heat 1 tablespoon olive oil over medium heat. Add the onion and cook until soft and translucent. Add the garlic and cook for 1 minute, making sure it does not burn.

4. Add the wine, salt, and white pepper, stir, and bring to a gentle simmer.

5. Add the clams, cover, and cook, checking after about 5 minutes to see if they're opening. When all the clams are open, remove them from the heat and top with parsley and lemon slices.

6. Place the bread slices on a baking sheet and brush them lightly with the remaining 4 tablespoons olive oil. Toast for 5 minutes, or until golden brown.

7. Serve immediately. You can store leftovers in an airtight container in the refrigerator for up to 3 days. Reheat in a skillet on the stovetop for best results.

PAIR IT WITH:

This dish pairs best with a sweet white wine or glass of White Peach Sangria (page 105).

Firefighter Chouriço

CHOURIÇO BOMBEIRO

Prep time: 5 minutes | Cook time: 10 minutes

If you're looking to impress your friends, make this showstopper. Traditionally, the chouriço is fired up in a footed clay dish made specifically for this recipe, but you can replicate this technique using a small baking dish fitted with a wire rack. **SERVES 4 TO 6**

½ cup grain alcohol,
  80 proof or higher

½ pound (about 1 link)
  chouriço, scored

1. Pour the alcohol into a footed Chouriço Bombeiro dish or a baking dish fitted with a wire rack.

2. Place the chouriço on the rack, and using a long match or lighter, carefully ignite the alcohol and let it burn for 8 to 10 minutes.

3. Using tongs, turn the chouriço, and continue to let the alcohol burn until the fire goes out.

4. Transfer the chouriço to a plate, slice, and serve.

HELPFUL HINT:

Have an oven mitt and a box of baking soda handy before lighting the alcohol. The flames can reach a few feet high, so make sure there is plenty of open space around the dish. Use the baking soda to douse the flames if you think they're getting too high.

Chouriço and Peppers Finger Sandwiches

SANDUÍCHES DE CHOURIÇO E PIMENTAS

Prep time: 20 minutes | **Cook time:** 1 hour

My mother showed me how to make this simple, delicious recipe and it's easily one of my most requested party foods. There's a lot of liquid in this dish to start (you may wonder if you're making soup!), but most of it will be absorbed or evaporate. These sandwiches are traditionally made with green bell peppers, but I use orange, red, or yellow because I prefer their sweetness. **MAKES 12 SANDWICHES**

2 tablespoons olive oil

1 bell pepper, cut into large dice

1 onion, cut into small dice

2 garlic cloves, minced

2 pounds ground chouriço

1 tablespoon Pimenta Moida (page 121)

12 ounces lager beer

6 ounces tomato sauce

12 Bread Rolls (page 127), cut in half

1. In a medium stockpot, heat the olive oil over medium heat. Add the pepper and onion and cook for 1 to 2 minutes. Add the garlic and stir for about 30 seconds.

2. Add the chouriço, Pimenta Moida, beer, and tomato sauce and stir to combine. Lower the heat to medium-low, cover, and simmer until the liquid is reduced by half, about 1 hour. Stir occasionally. The meat will be very moist but not soupy.

3. Remove from the heat. Stuff the rolls with the chouriço and pepper mixture and serve.

HELPFUL HINT:

Stuff the buns right before you plan to eat them. These sandwiches can sit out at room temperature for a party, but once they're stuffed they don't refrigerate well.

Stuffed Crepes
CREPES RECHEADOS

Prep time: 5 minutes | Cook time: 10 minutes

Here is a classic example of how Portugal has adapted cuisine from another culture and made it their own. Crepes are popular in trendy restaurants throughout Portugal, and they're a great way to use up leftovers like Chouriço and Peppers (page 26) at home. This recipe is for savory crepes, but for a dessert variation, fill them with strawberries and whipped cream.
SERVES 4 TO 6

¾ cup unbleached flour
1 teaspoon sugar
¼ teaspoon baking powder
¼ teaspoon baking soda
¼ teaspoon kosher salt
1 large egg

1 cup milk, at room
   temperature
1 tablespoon butter, melted
Margarine, for cooking

Leftover Chouriço
   and Peppers Finger
   Sandwiches (page 26),
   shredded Pot Roast
   (page 78), or Pulled Pork
   (page 75)

1. In a medium bowl, whisk together the flour, sugar, baking powder, baking soda, and salt and set aside.

2. In a small bowl, beat together the egg, milk, and melted butter. Add to the flour mixture and stir to combine.

3. In a small nonstick skillet over medium heat, lightly coat the pan with margarine.

4. Pour 2 tablespoons batter into the skillet and swirl the pan to coat the bottom with batter. Let cook until opaque, about 30 seconds. Use a spatula to lift the crepe off the hot pan, and then use your fingers to flip it. Cook for another 30 seconds, then transfer the crepe to a plate and cover with a kitchen towel. Repeat with the rest of the batter, making sure to coat the pan with margarine before cooking each crepe.

5. Reheat the filling in a large saucepan over medium heat. Spoon the filling into each crepe and roll it up. Serve immediately.

HELPFUL HINT:
You can store unfilled crepes, stacked with wax or parchment paper between each, in an airtight container in the freezer for up to 2 months. To use, let them come to room temperature and fill with your choice of ingredients.

CHAPTER THREE

Vegetables and Sides

Traditional Portuguese cuisine calls for two starchy side dishes to be served alongside a protein. One will usually have rice, and the other will include potatoes. A simple green salad is also popular and is frequently served on the same plate as the main dish.

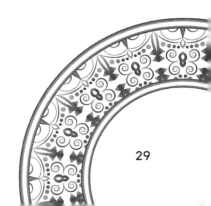

Roasted Chouriço and Potatoes (page 37)

Tomato Rice

ARROZ DE TOMATE

Prep time: 5 minutes | Cook time: 20 minutes

It's pretty common in Portuguese cuisine to serve potatoes and rice as the two starchy side dishes with a protein. This rice recipe goes with many entrées. **SERVES 4 TO 6**

---

3 tablespoons lard or
   bacon fat
1 medium onion, diced
4 garlic cloves, minced

4 Roma tomatoes, peeled
   and diced, and their juice
2½ cups chicken stock
1 cup long-grain rice

¼ teaspoon freshly ground
   white pepper
1 pinch kosher salt, plus
   more as needed

1. In a medium saucepan, melt the lard over medium heat. Add the onion and cook until soft, 3 to 4 minutes. Add the garlic and cook for 1 minute. Add the tomatoes, stir to combine, and bring to a simmer, about 1 minute.

2. Add the chicken stock and bring to a boil. Add the rice, white pepper, and salt, and stir to combine. Lower the heat to medium-low, cover, and cook for 20 minutes. Stir, and add salt to taste.

WHEN IN PORTUGAL:

This dish originated in warm Alentejo because of the ripe red tomatoes the region produces. If you're lucky enough to have farm-fresh tomatoes, please use them.

Fried Whole Potatoes

BATATAS FRITAS INTEIRAS

Prep time: 10 minutes | Cook time: 15 to 20 minutes

These crunchy delights are often paired with roasted beef, pork, or goat, and they can be used in Roasted Chouriço and Potatoes (page 37). You can also pile them high on a plate and serve as petiscos. They are especially lovely when topped with Fish Sauce (page 118) or Onion Medley (page 122).
SERVES 4 TO 6

---

2 quarts vegetable or peanut oil	10 to 12 extra small white or yellow potatoes, peeled	Kosher salt

1. In a large heavy-bottomed Dutch oven, heat the oil to 325°F.

2. Soak the potatoes in water for 2 to 3 minutes and dry thoroughly.

3. Line a plate with paper towels.

4. Slowly lower half the potatoes into the oil, being careful not to overcrowd them, and fry for 3 minutes without letting them brown. Adjust the heat as needed to keep the temperature at 325°F.

5. Transfer the fried potatoes to the lined plate. Repeat with the remaining potatoes.

6. Increase the temperature of the oil to 375°F. Fry the potatoes again, until lightly browned, cooking them in batches to avoid overcrowding, 5 to 6 minutes. Transfer to the lined plate. Repeat with the remaining the potatoes. Toss with salt and serve.

PAIR IT WITH:
These potatoes make a great snack paired with a glass of White Peach Sangria (page 105).

Thick-Cut Potato Chips
BATATAS FRITAS GROSSAS

Prep time: 10 minutes | **Cook time:** 10 to 15 minutes

These chips forever changed my husband's idea of French fries. Fry them to order and place them directly next to the protein you're serving so they'll soak up any sauces or juices. **SERVES 4 TO 6**

---

2 quarts canola oil

6 russet potatoes, peeled and cut into ⅛-inch slices

Kosher salt

1. In a large heavy-bottomed Dutch oven, heat the oil to 375°F.

2. Soak the potatoes in water for 2 to 3 minutes and dry thoroughly.

3. Line a plate with paper towels.

4. Slowly lower one-quarter of the potatoes into the oil, being careful not to overcrowd them, and fry for 5 to 6 minutes, until golden brown. Adjust the heat as needed to keep the temperature at 375°F.

5. Transfer the fried potatoes to the lined plate. Repeat with the rest of the potatoes. Toss with salt and serve immediately.

Taro Root with Onion Medley

INHAMS COM CEBOLADA

Prep time: 20 **minutes** | **Cook time:** 1 **hour**

Taro root really shines when you pair it with Onion Medley (page 122). Adding salt cod further elevates this recipe. This dish is great to have on the table when your vegetarian friends come for dinner. **SERVES 2 TO 4**

1½ pounds taro root, punctured several times with a fork

1 tablespoon kosher salt
¼ cup olive oil
2 fresh tomatoes, diced

2 cups Onion Medley (page 122)

1. Place the taro root in a large stockpot, and cover with 8 quarts water. Add the salt and bring to a boil over high heat. Lower the heat to medium-low, cover, and simmer until the taro is fork tender, about 45 minutes.

2. Set the taro aside until cool enough to peel. Then peel, cut into thick slices, and set aside.

3. In a large heavy-bottomed skillet, heat the olive oil over medium-high heat. Add the taro root slices and cook until golden brown. Turn the slices and continue to cook until golden brown. Add the tomatoes and cook for 5 minutes.

4. Add the Onion Medley, and fold into the taro root. Cook until heated through.

5. Serve warm.

EASY SUBSTITUTION:

Taro root can be found near the potatoes and yams in your local grocery store; they are tan and hairy. Select the smallest available, which should be about the size of a golf ball. If you can't find taro root, use russet potatoes or yams.

Baked Beans

FEIJÃO ASSADO

Prep time: 10 minutes, plus 12 hours to soak | Cook time: 2 hours

Fabulous paired with pork, this creamy, savory bean recipe is unlike any American-style baked bean dish and is great to bring to a potluck. Because most of the cooking is done on the stovetop, the beans are very tender. Chouriço provides a texture contrast. **SERVES 6 TO 8**

---

1 pound dried navy beans, soaked for 8 to 12 hours and drained

1 medium onion, diced

2 garlic cloves

½ teaspoon kosher salt, plus more as needed

6 ounces tomato sauce

1 heaping tablespoon Pimenta Moida (page 121)

½ pound chouriço, peeled and sliced

1-inch piece salt pork (or 3 slices thick-cut bacon, nonsmoky flavor)

½ teaspoon Portuguese All Spice (page 123) or paprika

1. In a large stockpot, mix together the beans, onion, garlic, and 8 quarts water. Bring to a boil over high heat. Lower the heat to medium-low, cover, and cook until the beans are very tender, stirring occasionally, about 1½ hours. Remove from the heat, add a pinch salt, and let sit, covered, for about 20 minutes.

2. Preheat the oven to 375°F.

3. Drain the beans, reserving 1 cup of the cooking water. Add the tomato sauce, Pimenta Moida, chouriço, salt pork, All Spice, and remaining ½ teaspoon salt, and stir to combine. Add the reserved cooking water and stir to combine. Transfer the beans to a 9-by-13-inch baking dish and bake for 1½ hours.

4. Serve immediately.

HELPFUL HINT:

Store leftovers in an airtight container in the refrigerator for up to 5 days. Reheat the beans by frying them in olive oil in a small skillet. They make a pretty wonderful breakfast.

Chickpeas with Tuna
ATUM COM GRÃO

Prep time: 10 minutes | **Cook time:** 25 minutes

Quick and easy, this tuna salad dish is great for picnics. It's the quintessential summertime food. **SERVES 2 TO 4**

¾ pound white potatoes, peeled and cut into large dice

1 tablespoon kosher salt, plus 1 teaspoon

⅓ cup red wine vinegar

½ small red onion, thinly sliced

⅓ cup olive oil

¼ cup chopped fresh flat-leaf parsley

½ teaspoon freshly ground white pepper

14 ounces high-quality canned tuna in oil

1 (15½-ounce) can chickpeas, drained and rinsed

⅓ cup (about 10) green olives

2 hard-boiled eggs, peeled and quartered

1. Put the potatoes in a large saucepan and cover with 6 quarts cold water. Add 1 tablespoon salt and stir to combine. Bring to a boil over high heat. Lower the heat to medium-low and cook until fork tender, about 20 minutes. Drain the potatoes, place in a large mixing bowl, and set aside.

2. In a small bowl, pour the vinegar over the onion and set aside to soak.

3. In another small bowl, whisk together the oil, parsley, remaining 1 teaspoon salt, and the white pepper.

4. Add the tuna, chickpeas, oil mixture, and vinegar-onion mixture to the potatoes, and top with the olives and hard-boiled eggs. Serve.

5. The longer this dish sits, the tastier it becomes. You can store in an airtight container in the refrigerator for up to 5 days.

PAIR IT WITH:
Serve this summer salad warm or chilled, and don't forget the wine. It pairs really well with a regional red wine from Alentejo, although most reds will do, and a slice of crusty bread.

Thanksgiving Stuffing
RECHEIO DE AÇÃO DE GRAÇAS

Prep time: 30 **to** 40 **minutes** | **Cook time:** 45 **minutes**

This stuffing with a Portuguese twist is one of the most requested recipes on my website. It's so tasty, you'll likely want to make it any time of the year.
SERVES 4 TO 6

---

12 Bread Rolls (page 127) or 2 loaves crusty Italian bread, torn into pieces
¼ cup olive oil
1 medium onion, diced

2 teaspoons Pimenta Moida (page 121) or 1 teaspoon Thai chili paste
2 garlic cloves, minced
½ pound ground chouriço

¼ cup turkey giblets, chopped (optional)
1 large egg, beaten
½ teaspoon Portuguese All Spice (page 123)
Kosher salt

1. Preheat the oven to 350°F.
2. Fill a large bowl three-quarters of the way with lukewarm water and submerge the bread. Set aside.
3. In a large skillet, heat the olive oil over medium heat. Add the onion and cook until translucent, about 5 minutes. Add the Pimenta Moida and garlic and cook for 1 minute. Add the chouriço and cook, stirring occasionally, until the sausage starts to render its fat and becomes crispy. Add the giblets, if using. Remove from the heat and set aside.
4. Squeeze the soaked bread between both hands until most of the water is removed. Add each piece of bread to the skillet with the chouriço mixture.
5. Lower the heat to low and cook the bread for about 10 minutes. Add salt to taste. Let the mixture cool for about 10 minutes.
6. Transfer the mixture to a large baking dish. Add the egg and All Spice and stir to combine.
7. Bake for 45 minutes to 1 hour, or until cooked through and the top is crispy.

HELPFUL HINT:
Because this dish is more labor-intensive than other recipes, consider doubling it. You can store half in an airtight container in the freezer for up to 4 months, and you'll be able to serve stuffing whenever you like. To reheat, thaw in the refrigerator overnight. Place the stuffing on a plate, cover with a damp paper towel, and microwave until hot.

Roasted Chouriço and Potatoes

BATATAS COM CHOURIÇO ASSADO

Prep time: 10 minutes | Cook time: 3 hours

This recipe is ridiculously easy to make. If you can't find chouriço, substitute chunks of pork marinated in Chouriço Marinade (page 116). For an extra burst of flavor, add some slices of hot peppers before cooking and garnish with parsley. **SERVES 2 TO 4**

---

6 ounces tomato sauce

6 ounces lager beer

3 tablespoons Pimenta Moida (page 121)

1 teaspoon kosher salt

½ teaspoon Portuguese All Spice (page 123)

2 garlic cloves, crushed and minced

8 medium potatoes, peeled

½ pound chouriço, cut into 10 pieces

1 small onion, thinly sliced

1. Preheat the oven to 375°F.

2. In a medium bowl, mix together the tomato sauce, beer, Pimenta Moida, salt, All Spice, and garlic.

3. Arrange the potatoes, chouriço, and onion in a baking dish. Pour the sauce over the mixture and stir to coat.

4. Cover the baking dish with foil, and roast for 2 to 2½ hours, or until the potatoes are fork tender. Remove the foil, turn the potatoes to coat with the sauce, and roast, uncovered, for 15 minutes more. Serve hot.

CHAPTER FOUR

Soups and Stews

Large families like my father's clan of eleven were commonplace in Portuguese Catholic homes, and feeding everyone on a daily basis almost always involved some sort of soup or stew. This selection is at the heart of a Portuguese family's table week in and week out. My family and many others have a big pot of soup or stew on the burner after church on Sunday, and it fills the house with the warm aroma of hearty goodness. What's left is served up throughout the week with crusty bread rolls.

Kale Soup (page 44)

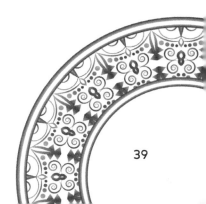

Dried Fava Stew

FAVAS GUISADAS

Prep time: 60 minutes, plus 24 hours to soak | Cook time: 1½ hours

Favas are feast food. If you have ever had the pleasure of visiting Portugal during feast season (late spring into early fall), you have likely seen people with Styrofoam bowls full of this delicious slow-cooked bean stew. Do note that the beans need to be soaked for 1 or 2 days before cooking (so be sure to plan ahead). **SERVES 6**

FOR THE FAVAS

1 pound dried fava beans

4 garlic cloves, crushed

1 tablespoon kosher salt

FOR THE STEW

1 teaspoon kosher or sea salt, divided

2 tablespoons olive oil

1 large onion, quartered and sliced

¼ cup chopped fresh flat-leaf parsley

4 garlic cloves, chopped

1 tablespoon Pimenta Moida (page 121)

½ teaspoon Portuguese All Spice (page 123)

¼ teaspoon freshly ground white pepper

12 ounces dry white wine

2 ounces tomato sauce

2 teaspoons red wine vinegar

1 dried bay leaf

TO MAKE THE FAVAS

Soak the dried fava beans with the garlic and salt for at least 1 day and up to 2 days, changing the water every 8 hours or so. Using a sharp knife, carefully peel off the top of the bean skin (about ⅛ inch) while leaving the rest of the bean intact.

TO MAKE THE STEW

1. In a large stockpot, mix together the favas, ½ teaspoon salt, and 8 quarts water, and bring to a boil over high heat. Lower the heat to medium and cook for 1 hour.

2. In a large Dutch oven or stockpot, heat the olive oil over medium heat. Add the onion and cook until translucent but not browned. Add the parsley and garlic and cook, stirring frequently, for 2 minutes. Add the Pimenta Moida, All Spice, and white pepper, stir to combine, and simmer for 1 minute.

3. Drain the fava beans and add the beans to the onion mixture. Add the wine, tomato sauce, vinegar, and bay leaf, and stir to combine. If the wine mixture does not quite cover the beans, add enough water to just cover them. Bring to a boil. Lower the heat to medium-low, cover, and simmer, stirring occasionally, until the favas are tender and the liquid has reduced by about two-thirds, about 1 hour. If the favas are not tender, add a few cups hot water and continue to cook until tender.

4. Add the remaining ½ teaspoon salt to taste. Serve hot.

HELPFUL HINT:

Traditionally, this stew is made without meat. Some like to add lard, chouriço, or both, which you can do at the end of step 2.

Green Fava Stew

FAVAS VERDES

Prep time: 30 minutes | **Cook time:** 1½ hours

Many of the ingredients my family used for cooking—grapes for jelly, kale for soup, and favas for this stew—were homegrown. I have vivid memories of my grandparents setting up chairs right out in the garden, my Vavó in her housecoat shelling fava beans for Sunday's lunch. **SERVES 4**

---

2 tablespoons olive oil

1 large onion, halved and sliced

4 garlic cloves, crushed

¼ cup chopped fresh flat-leaf parsley

½ pound chouriço, peeled and thinly sliced (hot or mild)

1 tablespoon Pimenta Moida (page 121)

¼ teaspoon Portuguese All Spice (page 123)

¼ teaspoon freshly ground white pepper

1 teaspoon kosher or sea salt

1 pound fresh or thawed shelled fava beans

12 ounces lager beer

4 ounces tomato sauce

4 large eggs (optional)

1. In a large Dutch oven, heat the olive oil over medium heat. Add the onion and cook until translucent but not browned. Add the garlic and parsley, and cook for 2 minutes, stirring frequently. Add the chouriço and cook for 2 minutes. Add the Pimenta Moida, All Spice, white pepper, and salt. Stir to combine, and simmer for 1 minute.

2. Raise the heat to medium-high. Add the fava beans, beer, and tomato sauce. If the liquid doesn't quite cover the beans, add enough water to just cover them. Bring to a boil. Lower the heat to medium-low, cover, and simmer for 45 minutes, stirring occasionally.

3. If using the eggs, create four small indentations in the beans, which will fill with liquid. Gently crack an egg into each indentation, cover, and simmer for an additional 15 minutes, or until the eggs are cooked to your liking.

4. Add salt to taste. Serve hot.

EASY SUBSTITUTION:

To use canned fava beans, rinse 2 (16-ounce) cans of beans and reduce the cooking time by half.

Octopus Stew

POLVO GUISADO

Prep time: 45 minutes | **Cook time:** 3 hours

This stew is made for dunking bread. The red wine tenderizes the tough octopus, and the long cook time melds the potatoes and broth into a rich combination. The preparation can be a bit messy and time-intensive, but this special dish is worth the effort. **SERVES 4**

---

1 small fresh or frozen and partially thawed octopus

2 tablespoons olive oil

1 medium onion, minced

2 garlic cloves, minced

1 tablespoon minced fresh flat-leaf parsley

1 tablespoon Pimenta Moida (page 121)

½ teaspoon Portuguese All Spice (page 123) or sweet paprika

1 cup red wine

4 ounces tomato sauce

1 pinch kosher salt (optional)

8 medium white potatoes, peeled and cut into 1-inch dice

1. Cut the octopus into 1-inch pieces. This process is easiest when the octopus is slightly frozen. If using fresh octopus, pop it in the freezer for about 30 minutes before handling.

2. In a medium stockpot, heat the olive oil over medium heat. Add the onion and cook until golden, about 5 minutes. Add the garlic and parsley, and cook for 2 minutes. Add Pimenta Moida and All Spice, and stir to combine.

3. Add the red wine, tomato sauce, and octopus, and bring to a boil. Lower the heat to medium-low, cover, and simmer, stirring occasionally, for 2 hours.

4. Add salt to taste. Some octopuses are naturally salty; others are not. Add the potatoes and stir to combine. Simmer until the potatoes are very soft and start to break down and thicken the stew, about 45 minutes.

5. Serve hot.

PAIR IT WITH:

I don't eat this dish without Bread Rolls (page 127) for sopping up the sauce, which is a big part of the experience. A nice glass of red wine goes well with this recipe, too, but a Wine Cooler (page 106) is even better.

Kale Soup

SOPA DE COUVES

Prep time: 2 hours 20 minutes | Cook time: 1½ hours

Sopa de Couves—or , affectionately, Sopinhas—is an iconic Portuguese soup. It is normally made on a Sunday morning and served later in the day with bread. Recipes vary by family and often depend on what's on hand or affordable. This recipe uses beans, potatoes, and kale, but my family recipe uses cabbage, split peas, and pureed beans as the base. **SERVES 4 TO 6**

FOR THE BEAN BASE

8 ounces dried pinto beans, rinsed and picked through for stones

1 garlic clove, crushed

FOR THE SOUP

½ pound bone-in beef shank

Kosher salt

½ pound (about 1 link) chouriço, cut into 1-inch slices

1 cup Portuguese kale or collard greens, stemmed and cut into ½-inch ribbons

1 cup chopped cabbage

2 tablespoons dried split peas

1 tablespoon Pimenta Moida (page 121)

6 medium white potatoes, cut into large dice

½ pound elbow macaroni

1 to 2 tablespoons vegetable oil (optional)

TO MAKE THE BEAN BASE

1. Soak the beans in water overnight. If you don't have time to soak, that's fine; the beans will just take a bit longer to cook.

2. In a 10-quart stockpot, mix together the beans, garlic, and 6 quarts water. Bring to a boil over medium-high heat. Lower the heat to medium-low, cover, and cook until the beans are very soft and popping open, about 2 hours. Check the water level several times as the beans are cooking, and add more if the water is low. Drain about half of the water, and use an immersion blender to puree the beans in the remaining cooking liquid.

TO MAKE THE SOUP

1. Add 6 quarts water to the pureed beans. Add the beef shank, a generous pinch salt, the chouriço, kale, cabbage, split peas, and Pimenta Moida, and stir to combine. Bring to a boil over high heat. Lower the heat to medium, and simmer until the kale and cabbage are soft, about 30 minutes.

2. Add the potatoes and cook until they are fork tender, about 30 minutes.

3. Add the elbow macaroni and cook until done, about 30 minutes.

4. Add the vegetable oil, if using. Add salt to taste.

5. You can store leftovers in an airtight container in the refrigerator for up to 5 days.

EASY SUBSTITUTION:
If you don't have time to soak and cook dried beans, use 1 (15½-ounce) can of pinto beans along with its liquid.

Lemon Chicken Soup

CANJA DE GALINHA

Prep time: 10 minutes | **Cook time:** 45 minutes

Chicken soup is the ultimate comfort food no matter what country you live in. Portugal's version is delicate and lemony. It is sometimes served with mint leaves and rice instead of pasta. **SERVES 4 TO 6**

1 tablespoon olive oil

1 small onion, cut into small dice

1 carrot, cut into small dice

1 garlic clove, minced

½ teaspoon kosher salt, plus more as needed

2 quarts chicken stock

1 chicken breast, chopped and shredded

2 egg yolks, beaten

Juice of 1 lemon

½ cup pastini pasta or stars

1 tablespoon chopped flat-leaf parsley

1. In a large stockpot, heat the olive oil over medium heat. Add the onion and carrot, and cook until tender. Add the garlic and salt, and cook for 1 minute. Add the chicken stock, stir to combine, and raise the heat to high to bring to a boil. Add the chicken and stir to combine.

2. In a small bowl, beat together the egg yolks and lemon juice. Slowly whisk in ¼ cup hot stock from the pot to temper the yolk. Slowly add the egg mixture back into the hot soup while stirring rapidly.

3. Add salt to taste.

4. Add the pasta, stir, and cook until fully cooked, 10 to 20 minutes. Add the parsley. Add salt to taste. Serve hot.

EASY SUBSTITUTION:

My mother tells me that my Vavó Olinda never actually used lemon in her soup or separated the egg white. To make my Vavó's version, replace the lemon with white vinegar and beat in the entire egg instead of just the yolk.

Beef Stew

CARNE GUISADA

Prep time: 10 minutes | **Cook time:** 1 hour 35 minutes

My Vavô Fernando loved a pot of beef stew on Sundays, though he rarely ate this dish while growing up on the island of Sao Miguel, where cows are reserved for dairy and beef is expensive. He worked hard and was able to move his family to the United States in the 1960s. In their new country, he and my Vavó Olinda worked in factories and saved enough to buy a home. To my Vavô Fernando, being able to eat beef stew, with its tender meat and hearty sauce, was a symbol of success—and also so delicious!

SERVES 4 TO 6

2 tablespoons olive oil

1 large onion, diced

1 garlic clove, crushed

1½ pounds stew beef, cut into cubes

½ pound Portuguese hot chouriço, sliced

1 heaping tablespoon Pimenta Moida (page 121)

½ teaspoon Portuguese All Spice (page 123)

6 medium potatoes, peeled and cut into large dice

12 ounces dry red wine (or lager beer)

4 ounces tomato sauce

Kosher salt

1. In a large Dutch oven, heat the olive oil over medium heat. Add the onion and cook for 2 minutes. Add the garlic and cook for 1 minute.

2. Add the beef and chouriço, and stir to combine. Add the Pimenta Moida and All Spice, and stir. Add the potatoes, wine, tomato sauce, salt, and 1½ cups water, and stir to combine. Lower the heat to medium-low, cover, and simmer, stirring every 10 minutes, until the potatoes are very tender, about 1½ hours. If the liquid gets low, add water, beer, or wine to make sure the potatoes stay submerged.

PAIR IT WITH:

Slices of crusty bread are perfect for sopping up the flavorful gravy. This meal calls for a nice glass of red wine to complement the richness of the meat.

Meat and Bean Stew
FEIJOADA

Prep time: 20 minutes, plus overnight to soak | **Cook time:** 1½ to 2 hours

This stew, originating in northern Portugal, shows up wherever there is a concentration of Portuguese immigrants. It's a particular favorite in Brazil. The ingredients are served in separate dishes, and diners assemble them to suit their taste. **SERVES 6 TO 8**

FOR THE BEANS

1 pound dried black beans

1 pound chouriço, sliced

½ pound paio
   sausage, sliced

2 oranges, peeled and
   sliced, divided

2 tablespoons olive oil

1 pound skirt steak, cut into
   2-inch-long thin slices

1 onion, coarsely chopped

4 garlic cloves, crushed

½ cup coarsely chopped
   fresh flat-leaf parsley

½ cup coarsely chopped
   fresh cilantro

1 tablespoon kosher salt

¼ teaspoon freshly ground
   black pepper

2 teaspoons Pimenta Moida
   (page 121)

½ teaspoon paprika

FOR THE GREENS

1 pound collard greens,
   ribs removed and cut into
   thin strips

1 teaspoon kosher salt

1 garlic clove, crushed

FOR THE RICE

2 chicken bouillon powder
   packets or cubes

1 teaspoon kosher salt

2 cups parboiled rice (such
   as Uncle Ben's)

TO MAKE THE BEANS

1. In a large stockpot, soak the beans in 6 quarts water overnight.

2. Drain the beans. Refill the stockpot with 6 quarts fresh water, add the soaked beans, and place over high heat.

3. Add the chouriço, paio, and the slices from one orange, and bring to a boil. Lower the heat to medium-low and let simmer.

4. While the beans are cooking, in a large skillet, heat the olive oil over high heat. Add the skirt steak and quickly sear on both sides, 7 to 8 minutes total. Transfer the steak to the stockpot with the cooking beans.

5. Lower the heat on the large skillet to medium, add the onion, and cook for 2 minutes. Add the garlic and cook for 2 minutes.

6. Put the onion, garlic, and any remaining oil into a blender. Add the parsley, cilantro, salt, pepper, Pimenta Moida, and paprika. Pour 1 ladleful of the bean

cooking water into the blender. Puree until smooth, then add to the stockpot of beans.

7. Raise the heat of the stockpot to medium-high and bring to a boil. Lower the heat to medium-low, stir, cover, and let simmer. Stir frequently over the next 90 minutes to 2 hours, until the bean water starts to take on the color of the black beans and look muddy. When the beans are tender, remove from the heat.

TO MAKE THE GREENS

In a separate large stockpot, mix together the collard greens, salt, garlic, and 6 quarts water. Bring to a boil over high heat. Lower the heat to medium-low and simmer until the greens are tender, about 30 minutes. Remove from the heat and set aside.

TO MAKE THE RICE

1. In a medium saucepan, mix together the bouillon, salt, and 6 cups water. Bring to a boil over high heat. Add the rice, stir, and bring to a boil again. Lower the heat to low, cover, and cook until the rice is tender, 25 to 30 minutes. Use a fork to fluff the rice, cover, and set aside.

2. Stir the beans and check the color of the water. If the water starts to take on the color of the beans and the beans are tender, drain the beans.

3. Divide the rice, collard greens, beans, meat and sausage, and remaining orange slices equally among serving bowls.

SUBSTITUTION TIP:
Paio is a smoked dried sausage that is commonly used in feijoada and is a combination of pork loin, salt, and capsicum peppers. If you can't find it, try using a high-quality beef jerky that has no sugar or added sweetness.

Chouriço and Peas
ERVILHAS COM CHOURIÇO

Prep time: 10 minutes | **Cook time:** 40 to 45 minutes

In the 1960s, when Portugal and its colonies were at war, Portugal fell into poverty, and many families moved to the United States. In 1966, my father, just 11 years old, made the journey by way of Canada before settling in Fall River, Massachusetts. His most vivid memory is his first meal with his Portuguese-Canadian family, Ervilhas com Chouriço: *Chouriço and Peas.*

SERVES 4 TO 6

---

3 tablespoons olive oil

1 medium yellow onion, quartered and sliced

½ pound chouriço, peeled and sliced

2 garlic cloves, minced

1 tablespoon Pimenta Moida (page 121)

¼ teaspoon Portuguese All Spice (page 123)

½ teaspoon kosher salt, plus more if needed

2 pounds fresh or frozen peas

12 ounces lager beer

½ cup tomato sauce

4 to 6 large eggs

1. In a large stockpot, heat the olive oil over medium heat. Add the onion and cook for 2 minutes. Add the chouriço and garlic, and cook for 3 to 4 minutes, taking care not to burn the garlic.

2. Add the Pimenta Moida, All Spice, and salt, and stir to combine.

3. Add the peas, beer, tomato sauce, and 2 quarts water, and stir to combine. Raise the heat to medium-high and bring to a boil. Lower the heat to medium-low, stir, cover, and cook, stirring occasionally, until heated through, 15 to 20 minutes.

4. With a large spoon, make 4 to 6 indentations in the peas to make room for the eggs to poach. Gently crack each egg into an indentation. Cover, and continue to cook for about 10 minutes. Add salt to taste.

5. Serve hot with fresh crusty bread.

EASY SUBSTITUTION:
If you'd like to make this recipe gluten-free, you can swap dry white wine for the beer.

HELPFUL HINT:
Each person should be served a whole egg with this meal, so be sure to adjust the number of eggs accordingly.

Green Soup
CALDO VERDE

Prep time: 30 minutes | **Cook time:** 1 hour to 1 hour 20 minutes

This rich and creamy soup is a great introduction to Portugal's cuisine and the perfect starter to any sit-down family meal. If you don't have an immersion blender (a worthy and not-too-expensive investment), you can very carefully ladle the hot soup into a blender and puree it in batches.
SERVES 6

---

5 pounds starchy potatoes, peeled and diced

1 medium onion, coarsely chopped

2 garlic cloves, crushed

1 teaspoon salt, plus more if needed

½ pound collard greens, cut into thin ribbons

½ pound hot or mild chouriço, peeled and thinly sliced

½ teaspoon freshly ground white pepper

1. In a 10-quart stockpot, mix together the potatoes, onion, garlic, salt, and 8 quarts water. Bring to a boil over high heat. Lower the heat to low, cover, and simmer until the potatoes are fork tender, about 45 minutes, checking frequently and adding water as needed to ensure the potatoes stay submerged.

2. With an immersion blender, carefully puree the potato mixture until completely smooth.

3. Add the collard greens, chouriço, white pepper, and enough water to fill the pot halfway. Bring to a boil over high heat. Lower the heat to low and simmer until the greens are tender, about 30 minutes. Add salt to taste. Serve hot.

HELPFUL HINT:

For a little extra spice, add 1 teaspoon Pimenta Moida (page 121) before pureeing the soup. Green soup is actually a milky white; the only color comes from the vibrant green of the collard greens and the dots of red chouriço.

Bean Soup
MOLHO DE FEIJÃO

Prep time: 2 hours 20 minutes | Cook time: 2 hours

Some call this soup Sopa de Feijão, *but, like my Vavó Olinda, I call it* Molho de Feijão. *Try it with Baked Beans (page 34).* **SERVES 6 TO 8**

FOR THE BEANS

16 ounces dried white navy beans, rinsed and picked through for stones

1 medium onion, diced

2 garlic cloves, crushed and minced

FOR THE SOUP

½ pound hot chouriço, peeled and sliced

5 to 6 medium potatoes, peeled and diced

2 ounces pork fat or uncured bacon (optional)

1 tablespoon Pimenta Moida (page 121)

Kosher salt

Freshly ground white pepper

8 ounces small-shell pasta

4 ounces tomato sauce

TO MAKE THE BEANS

In a 10-quart stockpot, mix together the beans, onion, garlic, and 8 quarts water. Bring to a boil over high heat. Lower the heat to low, cover, and cook until the beans are tender, 1½ to 2 hours. Check several times, and add water just to cover the beans, if needed.

TO MAKE THE SOUP

1. Add enough water to the beans to fill the stockpot halfway. Add the chouriço, potatoes, pork fat (if using), Pimenta Moida, a generous pinch salt, and the white pepper, and stir to combine. Raise the heat to medium-high and bring to a boil. Lower the heat to medium-low, cover, and cook, stirring frequently, until the potatoes are tender, about 30 minutes.

2. Add the pasta and cook, stirring frequently, for 30 minutes.

3. Add the tomato sauce and stir to combine. Add salt to taste. Serve hot.

4. You can store leftovers in an airtight container in the refrigerator for up to 5 days.

EASY SUBSTITUTION:

You can use any white bean for this recipe, but my Vavó always said the smallest white bean you can find will produce the smoothest broth.

Holy Ghost Soup
SOPA DE ESPIRITO SANTO

Prep time: 30 minutes, plus 45 minutes to rest | Cook time: 1½ hours

Every year, my church holds a lottery to determine the six mordunes *for the year. Mordunes are the families who host parishioners in their home to say the rosary in honor of the Holy Ghost each spring. The families open their home for prayer and refreshments each night for seven days. The week culminates in a celebration mass and dinner. When I was 12, my family was chosen. The women in my family made this soup as part of the celebration dinner. This recipe is my updated version of that iconic Azorean soup.*

SERVES 8

1 large onion, cut into quarters

4 garlic cloves, crushed

2 dried bay leaves

1 cinnamon stick (optional)

3 sprigs fresh mint, divided

1 tablespoon Pimenta Moida (page 121)

4 to 5 dried Jamaican allspice berries

1 cup Vinho Verde

2 bone-in, skin-on chicken leg quarters

1 bone-in beef shank

2 to 3 pounds beef brisket

½ pound morcela sausage, scored (optional)

½ pound chouriço, scored

2 tablespoons tomato paste

2 tablespoons red wine vinegar

1 tablespoon salt

8 medium potatoes, peeled and cut into quarters

1 pound collard greens, ribs removed and cut into 1-inch ribbons

½ head cabbage, cored and chopped

6 Bread Rolls (page 127), cut into chunks and set out to air dry

4 tablespoons salted butter, at room temperature

1. Lay out a large piece of doubled cheesecloth. Place the onion, garlic, bay leaves, cinnamon stick (if using), 1 sprig mint, Pimenta Moida, and allspice berries onto the cheesecloth. Carefully wrap up the ingredients and create a sachet by pulling up each corner of cheesecloth and tying them together with a long piece of baker's twine.

2. Tie one end of the sachet to the handle of a 10-quart stockpot for easy retrieval later. Put the Vinho Verde in the stockpot. Lower the sachet into the Vinho Verde and bring to a simmer over medium heat.

3. Add the chicken, beef shank, brisket, morcela (if using), and chouriço, and cover with water. Raise the heat to high, and add the tomato paste, vinegar, and salt. Stir to combine and bring to a boil. Lower the heat to low, cover, and simmer, stirring occasionally, for about 45 minutes.

4. Check the water level and add more if needed. Raise the heat to high. Add the potatoes, collard greens, and cabbage, and bring to a boil. Lower the heat to medium-low, and simmer until the greens and potatoes are tender, about 45 minutes. Add salt to taste.

5. In 2 or 3 large, deep serving dishes, arrange the bread and the remaining mint leaves. Ladle the broth from the soup over the bread. Cover and let sit for about 45 minutes, until the bread has soaked up all the broth.

6. Remove the sachet from the stockpot. Remove each piece of meat and sausage, cut into chunks, and return the meat to the pot. Cover with the remaining broth. Dot the meat with butter, and stir to combine. Cover and let sit.

7. Ladle the bread and broth into bowls, and top with the assorted meats. Serve hot.

WHEN IN PORTUGAL:
In the Azores, some variations of this soup include beef livers, whole chickens, and goat meat. Feel free to make this dish your own by adding or substituting ingredients you have on hand.

CHAPTER FIVE

Seafood

Seafood is one of the main ingredients of Portuguese cuisine—and not only because half of Portugal borders the Atlantic Ocean. The 10 islands off the coast were important points on the country's historical spice trade route. Over the centuries, the sea allowed Portugal to expand the flavor profile of its cuisine.

Shrimp Mozambique (page 60)

Stuffed Quahogs
AMÊIJOAS GRANDES RECHEADOS

Prep time: 20 minutes | **Cook time:** 40 minutes

This classic recipe for quahogs is a favorite in the seaside communities of Portugal. Try it as an appetizer bathed in butter, or top it with hot sauce.
SERVES 4 TO 8

---

4 large quahogs or large little neck clams

Kosher salt

2 tablespoons olive oil

8 tablespoons butter, divided

1 large onion, cut into small dice

1 red bell pepper, cut into small dice

3 garlic cloves, minced

¼ cup chouriço, cut into small dice

2 tablespoons minced fresh flat-leaf parsley

1 heaping tablespoon Pimenta Moida (page 121)

5 day-old Bread Rolls (page 127) or day-old Italian bread

¼ teaspoon Portuguese All Spice (page 123)

1 large egg, beaten

4 tablespoons butter, sliced into pads for topping

1 lemon, cut into wedges

1. Preheat the oven to 375°F.

2. Scrub the quahogs and soak them in a large bowl of salted water for 10 to 20 minutes.

3. Bring a medium stockpot of water to a boil over high heat. Add the quahogs and a pinch salt, cover, and bring to a boil. Cook until all the quahogs have opened. Throw away any that don't open. Reserve the liquid. Remove the meat from the shells and set aside the shells. Chop the quahog meat and set aside.

4. In a 10-inch skillet, heat the olive oil and 4 tablespoons butter over medium heat. Add the onion and cook until translucent. Add the bell pepper and cook 2 to 3 minutes. Add the garlic and cook for 1 minute. Add the chouriço and parsley, and cook until the fat is rendered from the chouriço, 3 to 4 minutes. Stir in the Pimenta Moida. Set aside and let cool.

5. Tear the bread into small pieces and place in a large bowl. Pour the cooking water from the quahogs over the bread, pressing the bread into the liquid to completely submerge it. Let the bread sit for a few minutes, then transfer the soaked bread to a colander set over a large bowl and drain the liquid. Using your hands, squeeze as much liquid out of the bread as you can, and place the bread pieces back into the bowl.

6. Add the quahog meat, the onion–bell pepper mixture, and the All Spice to the bread, and mix it together with your hands.

7. Add salt to taste. Add the egg and mix until completely combined.

8. Place the reserve quahog shells on a baking sheet. Spoon about ¼ cup of the stuffing into the shells, mounding the stuffing. Cover the baking sheet loosely with nonstick aluminum foil and bake for 20 minutes. Remove the foil, and bake for 20 minutes more. Serve hot with 1 tablespoon butter and a drizzle of lemon on each of the stuffed quahogs.

HELPFUL HINT:
You don't have to refrigerate these right away, so they're great to bring to work or school for lunch. Wrap them tightly in plastic wrap and reheat in a microwave oven.

Shrimp Mozambique
CAMARÃO MOÇAMIQUE

Prep time: 20 minutes | **Cook time:** 20 minutes

Shrimp Mozambique, a lemony, spicy peel-and-eat shrimp dish, is perfect party fare. You can use extra-large shrimp or prawns and serve it as a delicious starter for a more formal dinner party. No matter how you serve it, be sure to include the broth. **SERVES 4 TO 6**

---

2 pounds medium-size, "easy-peel" deveined raw shrimp

1 teaspoon kosher salt, divided

¼ cup olive oil

1 large onion, quartered and sliced

2 tablespoons salted butter

8 garlic cloves, sliced

2 packets Azafrán seasoning or 5 to 6 tendrils saffron

12 ounces lager beer

¼ cup chopped fresh flat-leaf parsley

1 tablespoon Pimenta Moida (page 121)

1 teaspoon piri piri or another hot sauce of your choosing

½ teaspoon Portuguese All Spice (page 123) or paprika

Juice of 1 lemon

1 teaspoon cornstarch

3 to 4 lemon slices, for garnish

3 to 4 parsley sprigs, for garnish

1. Place the shrimp on a plate and sprinkle with ½ teaspoon kosher salt.

2. In a large stockpot, heat the olive oil over medium heat. Add the onion and butter, and cook until soft, about 10 minutes. Sprinkle with a pinch salt. Add the garlic and cook for 1 minute. Add the Azafrán seasoning and stir to combine.

3. Pour the beer into the pan, and deglaze by scraping up the bottom of the pan with a wooden spoon. Add the parsley, Pimenta Moida, piri piri, All Spice, and lemon juice, and stir to combine. Raise the heat to medium-high, stir in 2 cups water, and bring to a simmer. Lower the heat to medium, add the shrimp, and cook until the shrimp turn pink, 5 to 10 minutes.

4. In a medium bowl, whisk together 1 cup water and the cornstarch. Add the mixture to the stockpot and cook, stirring frequently, for 5 minutes.

5. Transfer the shrimp to a serving platter, and garnish with lemon slices and parsley sprigs.

Limpets and Risotto

LAPAS COM ARROZ

Prep time: 2 minutes | **Cook time:** 30 minutes

Once a year, in midsummer, my mother took us, with my Vavó Olinda and Vavô Fernando, to dive for lapas. I hoped to reemerge from the water with a rock piled high with limpets. My Vavô would be ready with his knife to pull them from the rock and drop them in a bucket of cold sea water. We would eat our fill of salty, sweet shellfish right there on the beach, and then my Vavó would make a rice dish with what was left. This dish is inspired by her and those long, magical summer days. **SERVES 4 TO 6**

---

2 pounds limpets, scrubbed

1 teaspoon sea salt, plus more if needed

2 tablespoons olive oil

2 tablespoons butter

2 shallots, minced

2 garlic cloves, minced

2 cups arborio rice

1 teaspoon Pimenta Moida (page 121)

6 cups seafood or vegetable stock, warmed

1 cup Vinho Verde

½ cup shredded Parmigiano-Reggiano cheese

¼ teaspoon freshly ground black pepper

1 teaspoon minced fresh flat-leaf parsley

1. Run each limpet under hot water and remove from the shell. Set aside.

2. In a large skillet, heat the salt, olive oil and butter over medium heat. Add the shallots and cook until soft, 3 to 4 minutes. Add the garlic and cook for 1 minute. Add the rice and continue to cook until the rice is golden brown. Add the Pimenta Moida and stir to combine.

3. Pour 1 ladleful of the seafood or vegetable stock into the rice mixture and stir constantly. When rice has absorbed most of the liquid, add another ladleful and repeat until all the liquid has been absorbed. If the rice is not yet tender, add more stock and continue to stir until tender.

4. Add limpets and stir for 2 minutes. Add Vinho Verde and stir until absorbed. Add cheese and stir to combine. Stir in salt and pepper to taste. Sprinkle with parsley and serve hot.

EASY SUBSTITUTION:
If limpets aren't available, try this recipe with mussels or small cherrystone clams.

Grilled Sardines

SARDINHA GRELHADA

Prep time: 2 minutes | Cook time: 20 minutes

Summer isn't summer without sardines cooking on the grill. Simple to prepare, these delicious little fish need no prep beyond washing and a bit of seasoning. Serve them with some Seared Corn Bread (page 126) and a cold glass of Vinho Verde. **SERVES 4 TO 6**

---

12 fresh or thawed
  sardines, rinsed
1 teaspoon vegetable oil

1 teaspoon Pimenta Moida
  (page 121)
½ teaspoon fine sea salt

Cooking spray
Fish Sauce (page 118)

1. In a large bowl, mix together the sardines, vegetable oil, Pimenta Moida, and salt with your hands, working the seasoning into the fish.

2. Set a gas grill to medium or set up a charcoal grill for indirect heat. Spray the grill rack with nonstick grill spray. Grill the sardines until the skin starts to break, about 10 minutes per side.

3. Transfer to a serving platter, drizzle Fish Sauce over the top, and serve.

HELPFUL HINT:

For easier grilling, consider purchasing an inexpensive grill basket with a handle for flipping.

Fish Fillets
FILLETS DE PEIXE

Prep time: 20 minutes | **Cook time:** 20 minutes

This simple dish highlights the delicate flavor of haddock. Fillets de Peixe is a favorite at restaurants and is often served family-style at weddings and celebrations. Fish Sauce (page 118) or Vinegar Sauce (page 119) are wonderful accompaniments and should be served on the side to preserve the crispiness of the fish. **SERVES 4 TO 6**

Juice of 3 lemons

2 cups all-purpose flour

1 teaspoon baking powder

1 teaspoon fine sea salt

½ teaspoon sugar

2 large eggs, beaten

2 pounds haddock,
   skin removed

2 quarts peanut oil or
   vegetable oil

1 lemon, cut into slices
   or wedges

1. Pour the lemon juice into a small bowl and set aside.

2. In a medium shallow bowl, mix together the flour, baking powder, sea salt, and sugar, and set aside.

3. In another medium shallow bowl, mix together the eggs and 1 cup water, and set aside.

4. Cut the fish into 4-inch portions, and set aside the portions on a large plate.

5. In a medium Dutch oven or deep skillet, heat the peanut oil over medium-high heat, until the end of a wooden spoon dipped into the oil causes bubbles to form.

6. Line a plate with paper towels. Line up the bowls of lemon juice, the flour mixture, and the egg mixture. Dip 1 piece of fish into the lemon juice, dredge it in the flour mixture, and dip it into the egg mixture. Let any excess egg drip off. Gently drop the fish into the oil and fry for 4 to 5 minutes, until golden brown. You should be able to fry 2 to 3 pieces at a time, but be careful not to crowd them in the pan. Repeat with the rest of the fish. Transfer the fish to the lined plate to drain. Garnish with lemon slices or wedges and serve hot.

PAIR IT WITH:

This fish is commonly served atop steamed rice and dotted with carrots and peas. A white wine, such as an Encruzado from the Dão area, works nicely with this dish.

Codfish Casserole

BACALHAU GOMES DE SÀ

Prep time: 45 minutes | **Cook time:** 1 hour 15 minutes

Salted codfish is the most iconic fish of Portugal, and this is the most iconic preparation. The perfect balance of tender sliced potatoes, salty cod, and a succulent Onion Medley (page 122) sauce, all finished with a drizzle of rich olive oil, makes this casserole the king of all codfish dishes. **SERVES 8**

---

2 pounds salt cod, deboned

4 pounds potatoes, peeled

1 teaspoon kosher salt

¼ cup olive oil, divided

Onion Medley (page 122)

2 eggs, hard-boiled
  and sliced

12 olives

1. Preheat the oven to 350°F.

2. In a large stockpot, bring 3 quarts water and the cod to a boil over high heat. Drain, refill the pot with 3 quarts water, and boil again. Drain and flake the cod into chunks. Set aside.

3. Place the potatoes and salt in another large stockpot, cover with water, and bring to a boil over high heat. When the potatoes are cool enough to handle, cut them as thinly as you can without breaking them. Set aside.

4. Pour 1 tablespoon olive oil into a 9-by-13-inch baking dish. Layer with one-third of the potatoes, one-third of the Onion Medley, and half the cod. Repeat with 1 tablespoon olive oil, one-third of the potatoes, one-third of the Onion Medley, and the remaining cod. To finish, layer with the remaining potatoes, then the remaining Onion Medley.

5. Drizzle with olive oil, cover with aluminum foil, and bake for 1 hour. Remove the foil and bake for 15 minutes.

6. Top with the sliced hard-boiled eggs and the olives, and serve.

HELPFUL HINT:

For an elegant preparation worthy of a dinner party, make individual-size casseroles for your guests.

Skillet Salt Cod

BACALHAU À BRÁS

Prep time: 20 minutes | **Cook time:** 30 minutes

Another restaurant favorite, this relaxed dish is either served on a plate or in individual skillets for a dressed-up presentation. The only accompaniment this skillet salt cod needs is a fresh roll and a good glass of wine. Try a white Albariño or a red Madeira. **SERVES 4 TO 6**

FOR THE FISH

1 pound salt cod, deboned

FOR THE POTATOES

½ cup olive oil, divided

6 medium new potatoes, parboiled, peeled, and cut into matchstick fries

Pinch sea salt

Onion Medley (page 122)

8 large eggs, well beaten

1 tablespoon minced fresh flat-leaf parsley, plus more for garnish

1 cup olives of your choice (optional)

TO MAKE THE FISH

In a large stockpot, bring 3 quarts water and the cod to a boil over high heat. Drain, refill the pot with 3 quarts water, and boil again. Repeat one more time. Drain and flake the cod into chunks. Set aside.

TO MAKE THE POTATOES

1. Line a large plate with paper towels.

2. In a large skillet, heat ¼ cup olive oil over medium heat. Add the potatoes and fry until golden, 5 to 7 minutes. Drain on the lined plate. Toss the potatoes with a pinch salt.

3. Discard the oil in the skillet. Add the Onion Medley and cook for 1 minute. Add the cod and continue to cook for 3 to 5 minutes. Add the fried potatoes and fold in to incorporate. Add the eggs and parsley, and stir to coat all the ingredients. Cook until the egg is almost set.

4. Garnish with additional parsley and olives (if using), and drizzle with the remaining ¼ cup olive oil. Serve hot.

Codfish Omelet Sandwich

TORTAS DE BACALHAU

Prep time: 5 minutes | **Cook time:** 5 minutes

Tortas are Portuguese sandwiches and a typical way to use leftovers. Add last night's dinner, in chopped-up bits, to a basic egg omelet and you have a pretty phenomenal sandwich filler. The olive oil rallies around the beaten egg and gives it a good bubbling fry that pairs well with American cheese. Stuffed into a fresh crusty bread roll, the combination is hard to beat.

MAKES 4 SANDWICHES

---

4 tablespoons olive oil, divided

2 cups chopped cod from Codfish Casserole (page 64), divided

6 large eggs, beaten, divided

Pinch salt

4 slices American cheese

4 Bread Rolls (page 127), each cut in half

1. In a 10-inch nonstick skillet, heat 2 tablespoons olive oil over medium heat. Add half the cod and cook until it's heated through and starting to caramelize, 1 to 2 minutes.

2. Add half the egg mixture, sprinkle with a small pinch salt, and cook until about three-quarters done, 3 to 4 minutes. Flip and cook until cooked through, about 1 more minute. Transfer to a plate and add two slices of cheese to one side of the omelet. Gently fold the cooked egg in half over the cheese and place in a bread roll.

3. Repeat to make a second sandwich. Serve hot.

Fried Horse Mackerel

CHICHARROS

Prep time: 5 minutes | **Cook time:** 30 minutes

Portuguese fish markets sell more than raw fish. The small family-owned market my loved ones patronized had Codfish Cakes (page 22), Stuffed Quahogs (page 58), and fish and chips made to order, which we ate with Vinegar Sauce (page 119). **SERVES 2 TO 4**

---

1 pound bone-in, skin-on
 horse mackerel
Kosher salt

Freshly ground
 black pepper
1 cup yellow cornmeal

½ cup vegetable oil
Pepper Sauce (page 120)
 (optional)

1. Cut the fish into 2 to 4 portions. Season with salt and pepper, and set aside.

2. In a large shallow bowl, mix together the cornmeal with a pinch each of salt and pepper. Dredge the fish in cornmeal and set aside.

3. Line a plate with paper towels. In a medium skillet, heat the vegetable oil over medium-high heat. Add the fish, skin-side down, and cook without disturbing, until the skin is seared, 3 to 4 minutes. Turn over the fish and repeat until golden. Transfer the fish to the lined plate.

4. Top with Pepper Sauce, if using, and serve hot.

EASY SUBSTITUTION:
Horse mackerel is very different from plain mackerel; it's smaller and has a lighter flavor. If you can't find it, try any hearty white fish (like fresh cod), making sure to keep the skin intact.

Salmon Pinwheels

CATA-VENTOS DE SALMÃO

Prep time: 20 minutes, plus 1 hour to rest | Cook time: 20 to 30 minutes

Salmon is not something you often find in Portugal, but this seafood stuffing surely is. If you prefer something more traditional, use a white fish instead. Serve the pinwheels with plain white rice or Tomato Rice (page 30). **SERVES 2 TO 4**

2 tablespoons olive oil

1 large onion, cut into small dice

1 red bell pepper, cut into small dice

2 garlic cloves, minced

2 tablespoons minced fresh flat-leaf parsley

1 heaping tablespoon Pimenta Moida (page 121)

¼ teaspoon Portuguese All Spice (page 123)

40 buttery crackers, crushed

¼ cup seafood stock, plus more if needed

4 tablespoons butter, melted

1 tablespoon Worcestershire sauce

Juice of 1 lemon

¼ teaspoon freshly ground black pepper

Sea salt

2 sea scallops, diced

2 large shrimp, diced

1 (2-pound) salmon fillet

1 lemon, cut into wedges

1. In a 10-inch skillet, heat the olive oil over medium heat. Add the onion and cook until translucent, about 2 minutes. Add the bell pepper and cook for 2 to 3 minutes. Add the garlic, parsley, Pimenta Moida, and All Spice, and cook for 2 to 3 minutes. Set aside.

2. In a large bowl, mix together the crackers, seafood stock, melted butter, Worcestershire sauce, lemon juice, and pepper. Add the bell pepper mixture and stir to combine. Add salt to taste. Add the scallops and shrimp, and mix gently with your hands. If the mixture sticks together when squeezed, it's ready for stuffing. If not, add more stock, a little at a time, until it sticks together.

3. Spread the stuffing in an even layer over the salmon. Roll up the salmon the long way, and wrap tightly in plastic wrap. Refrigerate for at least 1 hour.

4. When you are ready to cook, preheat the oven to 350°F. Line a baking sheet with parchment paper. Unwrap the salmon roll and cut it into 1½-inch slices. Place the pinwheels on the prepared sheet. Roast for 20 to 30 minutes, or until the fish is cooked through.

5. Serve hot with lemon wedges on the side.

HELPFUL HINT:

If you can't find one two-pound salmon fillet, use two or more smaller fillets. Just divide the stuffing between them and roll them up as instructed.

EASY SUBSTITUTION:

You can also use the stuffing in large butterflied shrimp.

CHAPTER SIX
Meat and Poultry

White meat like pork and chicken have been the mainstays of Portuguese cuisine for centuries. Cattle have been mainly for milk production, and beef was typically used for celebratory cooking because it was more expensive. However, as the economy in Portugal has stabilized, beef has risen in popularity, both in restaurants and at home. In this chapter, you'll find dishes that highlight all three.

Piri Piri Chicken (page 83)

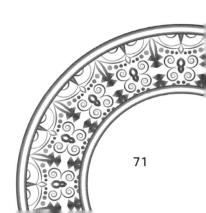

Alentejo-Style Roasted Cubed Pork with Little Necks

CARNE PORCO ALENTEJANA

Prep time: 30 minutes, plus overnight to marinate | **Cook time:** 1½ hours

One of Portugal's most popular party dishes is made with inexpensive pork and potatoes, making it perfect for feeding a crowd. But fresh clams are key to this dish hailing from the Alentejo region of Portugal. **SERVES 4 TO 6**

1 (2-pound) pork loin, trimmed and cut into 1-inch cubes

2 teaspoons kosher salt

2 cups dry white wine

10 garlic cloves, crushed

¼ cup minced fresh flat-leaf parsley

2 tablespoons tomato paste, divided

1 tablespoon Pimenta Moida (page 121)

2 teaspoons piri piri or another hot sauce of your choosing

1 teaspoon Portuguese All-Spice (page 123) or paprika

½ teaspoon freshly ground white pepper

1 dried bay leaf, crushed

4 pounds little neck clams, scrubbed

1 quart canola or peanut oil, for frying

2 pounds white potatoes, peeled, cut into 1-inch cubes and patted dry

¼ cup olive oil

1 large onion, diced

1 cup diced tomatoes

½ cup vegetable oil

½ lemon, sliced

½ cup olives of your choice

NIGHT BEFORE PREPARATION

1. In a large bowl, toss the pork with the salt and set aside.

2. In a large glass bowl, mix together the wine, garlic, parsley, 1 tablespoon tomato paste, Pimenta Moida, piri piri, All Spice, white pepper, and bay leaf. Add the pork and mix together to fully coat. Cover with plastic wrap and refrigerate overnight.

THE DAY OF COOKING

1. Set a colander over a large bowl and strain the pork. Reserve the marinade, and let the pork dry a bit. Remove the garlic from the strained ingredients in the colander and set aside.

2. Pour 1 quart water into a medium saucepan and bring to a boil over high heat. Add the clams, cover, and steam until all the clams have opened, about 10 minutes. Discard any clams that have not opened. Reserve 1 cup cooking water.

3. Line a plate with paper towels. In a medium saucepan or Dutch oven, heat the canola oil over high heat until the end of a wooden spoon inserted into the oil causes bubbles to form. Fry the potatoes in four batches until golden. Transfer each batch to the lined plate and season lightly with salt.

4. In a large saucepan, heat the olive oil over medium heat. Add the onion and cook for 10 minutes. Add the diced tomatoes and the remaining 1 tablespoon tomato paste. Cook for about 10 minutes, stirring occasionally. Add the reserved cooking water and the reserved marinade, and bring to a boil. Let boil until the liquid is reduced by half, about 45 minutes.

5. In a large heavy-bottomed skillet or cast-iron skillet, heat the vegetable oil over high heat. Add the pork and brown the meat in four batches, turning to ensure a good sear on each side, about 10 minutes per batch. Transfer each batch to a plate and set aside. Add the reserved garlic to the skillet and cook for 1 to 2 minutes.

6. Add the pork back into the skillet with the garlic. Lower the heat to medium-low, add the tomato mixture, and stir to combine. Cook, stirring frequently to ensure nothing sticks to the bottom of the pan, for about 15 minutes.

7. If the skillet with the pork is big enough, add the fried potatoes and gently fold them into the meat mixture, taking care not to mash or break up the potatoes. If the skillet is not big enough, transfer the meat and fried potatoes to a large bowl and fold them together. Reserve six clams and set aside. Add the remaining little necks to the meat and potatoes, and gently fold them together. Transfer the mixture to a large serving platter. Place the reserved clams over the top, and garnish with lemon slices and olives. Serve hot.

Pan Fried "Pork Chomps"

COSTELETA DE PORCO FRITA

Prep time: 5 minutes | **Cook time:** 20 minutes

In Portugal, meat is always cooked well done (medium rare is almost unheard of), and this recipe, dubbed "Pork Chomps" by my son in kindergarten, highlights how delicious well done can be. When shopping for pork chops, look for the thinnest cuts because they soak up all the seasoning.
SERVES 2 TO 4

---

4 thinly sliced, bone-in
  pork chops
6 garlic cloves, crushed

½ cup lager beer
2 tablespoons Pimenta
  Moida (page 121)

1 teaspoon kosher salt
2 tablespoons olive oil or
  vegetable oil

1. Place the pork chops in a medium bowl. Add the garlic, beer, Pimenta Moida, and salt, and stir to coat. Cover and refrigerate for at least 10 minutes or up to 1 day.

2. When ready to cook, let the pork sit at room temperature for 20 minutes.

3. In a large heavy-bottomed nonstick skillet, heat the olive oil over medium-high heat. Using tongs or a fork, remove the pork chops from the marinade, letting any excess marinade drip into the bowl. Place the pork chops in the skillet and cook until dark golden brown, 7 to 10 minutes. Flip the pork chops and continue to cook until dark golden brown, about 7 to 10 minutes. While the chops are cooking, use a slotted spoon to remove the garlic and some of the Pimenta Moida from the marinade and place it on the chops. Watch carefully to make sure the garlic doesn't burn.

4. Serve hot.

PAIR IT WITH:

At home, we serve these chops with steamed rice and green beans, but more traditional sides are rice and fried potatoes.

Pulled Pork

CAÇOILA

Prep time: 20 minutes | **Cook time:** 1 hour

Feast season, from late spring to early fall, is a very special time in Portugal. At this celebration of religious faith and Portuguese culture and traditions, villages come together to mingle, listen to music, and eat specialties like Caçoila, savory pulled pork that's stuffed into fresh Portuguese bread. Try serving this dish as a main course over steamed white rice with potatoes on the side. **SERVES 4 TO 6**

FOR THE DRY RUB

2 tablespoons kosher salt

2 teaspoons paprika

1 teaspoon granulated garlic

1 teaspoon granulated onion

1 teaspoon red pepper flakes

½ teaspoon ground cinnamon

¼ teaspoon ground turmeric

1 dried bay leaf, crushed

FOR THE PORK

4 pounds boneless pork butt or boneless pork shoulder, cut into pieces

1½ cups lager beer

1 large onion, diced

10 garlic cloves, minced

2 tablespoons Pimenta Moida (page 121)

2 tablespoons olive oil

Peel of 1 orange

TO MAKE THE DRY RUB

In a small bowl, mix together the salt, paprika, granulated garlic, granulated onion, red pepper flakes, cinnamon, turmeric, and bay leaf.

TO MAKE THE PORK

1. In a large bowl, mix together the spice rub and the pork. Cover with plastic wrap and refrigerate for at least 6 hours and up to 24 hours.

2. In a 6-quart slow cooker, mix together the seasoned pork, beer, onion, garlic, Pimenta Moida, olive oil, orange peel, and ¾ cup water. Set the slow cooker on low and cook for 6 hours.

3. Remove each piece of pork and shred into ½-inch chunks, making sure to discard any large fatty pieces, and return the chunks to the cooking liquid. Turn the slow cooker to warm, and let the pulled pork absorb the savory cooking liquid for about 20 minutes before serving.

Boiled Dinner

COZIDO

Prep time: 10 minutes | **Cook time:** 1½ to 2 hours

Residents of the Portuguese village of Furnas make a one-of-a-kind espresso by mixing their powdered instant coffee with the water from nearby hot mineral springs. My cousin would lower a sack of meats, potatoes, and vegetables into one of these springs. When we returned to the spring several hours later, we retrieved a fully cooked feast. This recipe is an easy variation on the dish, no hot spring required. **SERVES 6**

---

1 (10-pound) smoked pork
  shoulder
8 white potatoes, cut
  halfway through

½ pound hot Portuguese
  chouriço, scored
3 large onions, peeled

½ head cabbage, cut in half
  with core intact
6 carrots, peeled
1½ cups lager beer

1. Keeping the mesh intact, rinse the pork shoulder and set aside.

2. In a large stockpot, place the ingredients in the following order: potatoes, pork shoulder, chouriço, onions, cabbage, and carrots. Add the beer and 2 quarts water.

3. Cover the pot and bring to a boil over high heat. Lower the heat to medium-low and cook at a low boil for 1½ to 2 hours. Remove the mesh from the meat and discard. Serve hot.

WHEN IN PORTUGAL:

In Portugal, Cozido is traditionally cooked in a hot mineral spring. If you want to come a little closer to that classic flavor, swap some of the plain water for mineral water.

Pork Cutlet Sandwich

BIFANA

Prep time: 10 minutes, plus overnight to marinade | **Cook time:** 10 minutes

You can get a Bifana sandwich almost anywhere Portuguese food is served, and it's a staple in any home cook's repertoire. Served on simple Bread Rolls (page 127) alongside Fried Whole Potatoes (page 31), this dish is a great lunch option. **MAKES 4 SANDWICHES**

---

4 thinly sliced petite pork cutlets, about ½ pound

1 tablespoon kosher salt

5 garlic cloves, sliced

½ cup white wine

1 teaspoon Pimenta Moida (page 121)

1 teaspoon paprika

¼ teaspoon freshly ground white pepper

2 dried bay leaves

Juice of 1 lemon

2 ounces lard

4 Bread Rolls, split (page 127)

4 pickled hot chile pepper strips (optional)

1. Place the cutlets in a large container with a lid. Season with the salt, and add the garlic, wine, Pimenta Moida, paprika, white pepper, bay leaves, and lemon juice. Cover and refrigerate overnight.

2. When ready to cook, in a medium skillet, heat the lard over high heat. Using tongs or a fork, transfer the cutlets to the skillet, letting the excess marinade drip into the container. Sear the cutlets for about 5 minutes on each side.

3. Place each cutlet in a Papo-seco roll and top with chile pepper strips, if using. Serve hot or at room temperature.

PAIR IT WITH:
This sandwich goes really well with a cold beer and a side of fries.

Pot Roast

CARNE ASSADA EM PANELA

Prep time: 30 minutes | **Cook time:** 1 hour

When preparing this dish, the meat should melt in your mouth and the potatoes should fall apart when punctured with a fork. I first dredge the meat in corn flour, which is finely ground corn. But you can substitute all-purpose flour, or use cornstarch in a pinch. **SERVES 4 TO 6**

FOR THE POT ROAST

1 (2-pound) beef
  chuck roast
1 cup corn flour or
  all-purpose flour
2 tablespoons kosher salt
12 small new potatoes

1 cup red wine
2 tablespoons tomato paste
1 dried bay leaf
2 pieces salt pork or
  3 slices bacon,
  cut into ½-inch pieces
6 garlic cloves,
  crushed, divided

4 tablespoons vegetable oil
4 medium carrots, trimmed
  and peeled
1 cup pearl onions
2 tablespoons Pimenta
  Moida (page 121)
2 teaspoons cornstarch

TO MAKE THE POT ROAST

1. Let the beef sit at room temperature for at least 20 minutes before preparation. Preheat the oven to 375°F. Place the corn flour in a large bowl.

2. Season the beef on all sides with the salt. Dredge the beef in the corn flour and shake off any excess. Set aside.

3. Using a fork, puncture the potatoes a few times and set aside.

4. In a small bowl, whisk together the wine and tomato paste. Add the bay leaf and set aside.

5. In a large Dutch oven, cook the salt pork over medium-high heat until the fat is rendered. Remove the salt pork and set aside. Add the garlic to the fat and cook until golden, 1 to 2 minutes. Remove the garlic and set aside.

6. Raise the heat to high, add the vegetable oil to the Dutch oven, and add the beef. Sear until the beef has a dark crust on each side, about 5 minutes per side. (It may get smoky, so be sure to use your kitchen vent.) Set the beef aside on a large plate.

7. Place the potatoes in the bottom of the Dutch oven, and top with the carrots and 2 garlic cloves. Sprinkle with salt. Place the beef on top of the vegetables and top with Pimenta Moida, the remaining 4 garlic cloves, and the pearl onions. Pour the red wine mixture slowly over everything.

8. Cover and roast for 45 minutes to 1 hour. Remove from oven and let rest, covered, for 15 minutes. Arrange the beef and vegetables on a large platter and set aside.

9. Strain the drippings from the Dutch oven into a small saucepan.

TO MAKE THE GRAVY

1. Place the saucepan with the drippings over medium heat.

2. In a small bowl, whisk together cornstarch and ¾ cup water until smooth. Slowly whisk the mixture into the heated drippings and bring to a boil, whisking constantly. If the mixture becomes too thick, add another ½ cup water and whisk until smooth. Add salt to taste.

3. Pour the gravy into a bowl and serve it with the pot roast and vegetables.

HELPFUL HINT:

For a more modern twist on this gravy (and one most traditional Portuguese chefs might not approve of), add some sautéed mushrooms and ½ cup port wine to the drippings before adding the cornstarch mixture.

Portuguese Steak
BIFE À PORTUGUESA

Prep time: 10 minutes | **Cook time:** 20 minutes

The way Portuguese restaurants and home cooks prepare their steak is a point of comparison and, sometimes, competition. Some cooks use a Basic Meat Marinade (page 117), and some tweak it, as I've done here, but the steak is always accompanied by some peppers and a fried egg. **SERVES 2**

---

2 (10- to 12-ounce) sirloin steaks

4 garlic cloves, crushed and sliced

½ cup lager beer

2 tablespoons Pimenta Moida (page 121)

½ teaspoon kosher salt

½ cup vegetable oil, divided

1 pickled chile pepper, cut in half and seeded

2 large eggs

1. Place the steaks in a medium glass bowl. Add the garlic, beer, Pimenta Moida, and salt, and stir to combine. Cover the bowl and refrigerate for at least 20 minutes or up to 1 day. Let sit at room temperature for 20 minutes before cooking.

2. In a large skillet, heat ¼ cup vegetable oil over high heat. Using tongs or a fork, transfer the steaks to the skillet, letting the excess marinade drip into the bowl. Sear the steak for 5 minutes on each side, or until the steaks reach the desired level of doneness. Set aside on plates tented with foil. Reserve the marinade and set aside.

3. While the skillet is still over high heat, use a slotted spoon to remove the garlic from the marinade and cook it for 1 minute. Add the marinade and cook until reduced by half, 4 to 5 minutes. Add the pickled pepper to the sauce and cook for about 30 seconds. Top the steaks with the sauce.

4. In a small nonstick skillet, heat the remaining ¼ cup vegetable oil over medium heat. Gently crack the eggs into the skillet and cook, using a metal spoon to pour the heated oil over the eggs as they cook.

5. To serve, place each steak on a separate plate. Place an egg on top of each steak, and drizzle some sauce over the top.

WHEN IN PORTUGAL:

This dish is traditionally paired with steamed white rice and Fried Whole Potatoes (page 31), along with a glass of red wine or cold beer. These steaks are great in a sandwich, too!

Skewered Beef

CARNE ESPETO

Prep time: 30 minutes | **Cook time:** 1 hour

In Fall River, Massachusetts, the Espirito Santo Church kicks off the Holy Ghost feast season every Memorial Day weekend. For decades, my father has walked in the big procession, which culminates in a feast. He and his sons-in-law assemble 3½-foot-long metal skewers of seasoned meat, roasted over a large open charcoal pit, as the rest of us snack on malasadas (fried dough) with the kids. For this recipe, use your own grill and a few smaller skewers. **SERVES 4 TO 6**

---

3 pounds beef roast, cut into 2-inch cubes

1 cup coarse kosher salt or sea salt

2 tablespoons granulated garlic

1 tablespoon red pepper flakes

1 tablespoon freshly ground black pepper

3 dried bay leaves, crushed

1. Light a charcoal grill with sections for direct and indirect heat.

2. Place the beef on the skewers and set aside.

3. In a medium bowl, mix together the salt, garlic, red pepper flakes, black pepper, and bay leaves. Sprinkle the mixture liberally on each skewer.

4. Place the skewers on the rack and grill over direct heat, turning frequently, until each side is seared. Move the skewers to indirect heat and grill, turning the skewers every 5 minutes, until the meat is done to your liking. Let the skewers rest for 10 minutes before serving.

PAIR IT WITH:
A cold draft beef is the perfect accompaniment to these skewers.

Chicken and Rice

FRANGO COM ARROZ

Prep time: 10 minutes | **Cook time:** 45 minutes

Comfort food is the name of the game with this gem of a recipe. An easy weeknight meal or one to serve on a casual Sunday afternoon, this dish is also easy to prepare in a slow cooker or a pressure cooker, which makes it great when you don't have a lot of time. **SERVES 4**

---

4 tablespoons olive oil

2 pounds bone-in, skin-on chicken legs, thighs, or both

1 large onion, diced

1 pound hot chouriço, peeled and sliced

3 garlic cloves, crushed

6 white potatoes, peeled and diced

2 cups medium-grain white rice

1 (6-ounce) can tomato sauce

¼ cup lager beer

2 tablespoons Pimenta Moida (page 121)

1 teaspoon kosher salt

½ teaspoon Portuguese All Spice (page 123)

1. In a large heavy stockpot, heat the olive oil over high heat. Add the chicken and sear on all sides, about 3 minutes per side. Set aside.

2. Lower the heat to medium, add the onion, and cook for 2 minutes. Add the chouriço and garlic, and sauté for 2 to 3 minutes. Add the chicken and stir to combine.

3. Raise the heat to medium-high. Add the potatoes, rice, tomato sauce, beer, Pimenta Moida, salt, All Spice, and 6 cups water, and stir to combine. Bring to a boil. Lower the heat to medium-low, cover, and cook, stirring frequently, until the potatoes are fork tender and the rice is fully cooked and has absorbed most of the liquid, about 30 minutes. Add salt to taste. Serve hot.

EASY SUBSTITUTION:

I use bone-in chicken here because it's more flavorful, but boneless chicken breast or thighs work well, too.

Piri Piri Chicken

FRANGO COM PIRI PIRI

Prep time: 20 minutes | **Cook time:** 1 hour

If you've ever visited Portugal, you probably noticed that the Portuguese are not afraid to fry food. This fiery chicken is a fine example. It's a great dish to bring to a potluck or to serve at a dinner party because you can make it ahead of time. **SERVES 4 TO 6**

4 bone-in, skin-on chicken thighs

4 chicken drumsticks

4 chicken wings

4 quarts vegetable oil or peanut oil, for frying

1 cup piri piri sauce

¼ cup olive oil

Juice of 1 lemon

1 teaspoon granulated garlic

½ teaspoon kosher salt

1. Let the chicken sit at room temperature for 20 minutes before cooking. In a heavy stockpot, heat the vegetable oil over medium-high heat.

2. Preheat the oven to 400°F. Line a baking sheet with parchment paper. Line a plate with paper towels.

3. In a large bowl, mix together the piri piri sauce, olive oil, lemon juice, granulated garlic, and salt, and set aside.

4. Pat dry the chicken with paper towels. If the end of a wooden spoon inserted into the oil causes bubbles to form, the oil is ready for frying.

5. Fry the chicken, four pieces at a time, until golden brown. Transfer the chicken to the lined plate. As soon as the next four pieces of chicken are frying, transfer the cooked chicken to the bowl with the sauce and toss to coat. Using tongs, remove the chicken, letting any excess sauce drip back into the bowl, and place on the prepared sheet. Repeat with all the chicken. Reserve any remaining sauce.

6. Roast the chicken for 20 minutes. Baste the chicken with the remaining sauce. Continue to roast for 10 minutes. The chicken is done when a thermometer inserted into the thickest part of the meat reaches 165°F. Serve hot.

EASY SUBSTITUTION:
If you can't find piri piri sauce at the store or online, use your favorite hot sauce instead.

Mozambique-Style Chicken
FRANGO À MOÇAMBIQUE

Prep time: 20 minutes | **Cook time:** 1 hour

Each year, I teach this recipe to a group of Portuguese language students at my high school alma mater. We invite teachers, staff, and students to enjoy the meal, and everyone simply adores the outcome. In the class, I always review the history of spices like saffron, which Portugal got from its former colony Mozambique, and the unique Azafrán spice, a blend of Mexican saffron, turmeric, garlic, and monosodium glutamate. **SERVES 4 TO 6**

2 pounds boneless, skinless chicken breast, cut into 1-inch slices

2 teaspoons kosher salt, divided

¼ cup olive oil

2 tablespoons salted butter

1 large onion, quartered and cut into slices

4 garlic cloves, sliced

2 packets Azafrán seasoning or 5 to 6 tendrils saffron

2 cups dry white wine

¼ cup chopped fresh flat-leaf parsley

1 tablespoon Pimenta Moida (page 121)

1 teaspoon piri piri or a hot sauce of your choosing

½ teaspoon Portuguese All Spice (page 123) or paprika

Juice of ½ lemon

1 teaspoon cornstarch

¼ cup black olives, for garnish

3 to 4 lemon slices, for garnish

3 to 4 parsley sprigs, for garnish

1. Place the chicken on a plate and sprinkle with 1 teaspoon kosher salt.

2. In a large heavy-bottomed skillet, heat the olive oil over medium-high heat. Add the chicken and sear on all sides, about 2 minutes per side. Transfer the chicken to a plate and set aside.

3. Lower the heat to medium-low. Add the butter and onion, and cook until soft, about 10 minutes. Sprinkle with the remaining 1 teaspoon salt, add the garlic, and cook for 1 minute. Add the Azafrán seasoning and stir to combine.

4. Add the wine and use a wooden spoon to deglaze the pan by scraping the browned bits from the bottom of the pan. Add the parsley, Pimenta Moida, piri piri, All Spice, and lemon juice, and stir to combine. Add the chicken, bring to a simmer, and cook for about 5 minutes.

5. In a small bowl, whisk together the cornstarch and ½ cup water until smooth. Add the mixture to the skillet and cook, stirring, for 5 minutes.

6. Transfer to a serving plate, and garnish with olives, lemons, and parsley.

HELPFUL HINT:

You can make this recipe as mild or spicy as you want with piri piri hot sauce. I usually make mine on the mild side and put the bottle of piri piri on the table, so people can use as much as they like.

CHAPTER SEVEN

Pastries and Desserts

These sweet treats are sure to inspire the baker in you. Custards, cinnamon-laced pastries, and lemon-flavored goodies are all common Portuguese dessert offerings.

Custard Tart Cups (page 92)

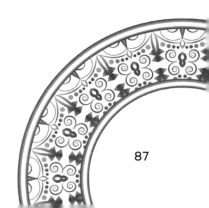

Flan Pudding with Caramel Sauce

PUDIM FLAN

Prep time: 10 minutes | **Cook time:** 35 minutes

Portugal's answer to crème brûlée is this creamy custard topped with an infused caramel. Pudim Flan is commonly enjoyed at the end of a meal with a hot cup of espresso or café Americano. I like to make this dessert in my fanciest, tallest Bundt pan for the maximum wow factor. If you're not a fan of nutmeg, you can use cinnamon instead. **SERVES 6 TO 8**

FOR THE SAUCE
1¼ cups sugar

FOR THE PUDDING
8 large eggs plus 2 large
  egg yolks

1¼ cups sugar
3 cups whole milk
1 cup light cream
1 tablespoon brandy

¼ teaspoon freshly
  grated nutmeg

TO MAKE THE SAUCE

1. Preheat the oven to 350°F.

2. In a small saucepan over medium heat, mix the sugar and ½ cup water. While the sugar is melting, tilt the pan in a circular motion, but do not stir. When the mixture turns a deep amber color, about 5 minutes, pour it into a high-sided metal Bundt pan, and tilt the pan to cover the bottom and sides lightly with the quickly hardening caramel. Place the Bundt pan in a 9-by-13-inch baking dish and set aside.

TO MAKE THE PUDDING

1. In the bowl of an electric mixer, whisk the eggs and egg yolks until they are a pale yellow color and frothy. Set aside.

2. In a 3-quart saucepan over medium-low heat, mix the sugar, milk, cream, and brandy, and whisk until the sugar dissolves. Set aside and let cool for a few minutes.

3. Pour about ½ cup hot milk mixture into the beaten eggs, whisking constantly. Slowly whisk in the remaining milk mixture.

4. Place a fine-mesh sieve over the Bundt pan and strain the mixture through it into the Bundt pan. Dust with freshly ground nutmeg.

5. Place the baking dish with the Bundt pan in the oven, and carefully pour very hot tap water into the baking dish until it is about three-quarters full, creating a water bath around the Bundt pan.

6. Bake for 35 minutes, or until a knife inserted into the thickest part of the flan comes out clean.

7. Remove the Bundt pan from the water bath and let cool for 20 minutes before putting it in the refrigerator to chill completely.

8. To remove the flan from the pan, gently loosen the sides of the pudding by running a butter knife around the edge of the pan, being careful not to disturb the design of the flan. Place a serving plate on top of the Bundt pan and quickly flip the plate and the Bundt pan upside-down together. Let all the caramel drip onto the pudding. Serve chilled.

9. You can store leftovers in an airtight container and refrigerate for up to 5 days.

EASY SUBSTITUTION:
This recipe calls for brandy, but port wine, vanilla, or lemon rind will all add wonderful flavors to this dessert.

Rice Pudding

ARROZ DOCE

Prep time: 5 minutes | Cook time: 45 minutes

Nothing could be more delicious than rice pudding. It's one of my mother's specialties, and she makes it all the time for her grandchildren, who devour it. For this recipe, do not use a nonstick pan or the rice will burn and ruin the recipe. **SERVES 4 TO 6**

---

3 cups whole milk, plus
  1 cup, if needed
Whole peel of 1 lemon
½ teaspoon kosher salt

1 cup medium-grain
  white rice
1 cup sugar
1 large egg yolk

½ teaspoon ground
  cinnamon

1. In a heavy-bottomed stainless-steel stockpot over medium-high heat, mix the milk, lemon peel, salt, and 1 cup water, and bring to a boil.

2. Add the rice, stir to combine, and bring back to a boil. Lower the heat to low, cover, and simmer, stirring gently and frequently, until the rice is very soft. If the liquid has been absorbed and the rice is not yet soft, add a little more milk and water and continue to cook. Do not scrape up the bits that have stuck to the bottom of the pot or brown bits of rice will end up floating in your pudding.

3. Once the rice is tender and most of the liquid has been absorbed, add the sugar and continue to cook on low, stirring frequently without scraping the bottom of the pan, until the liquid is absorbed again, 5 to 10 minutes. (The mixture will liquify as the sugar melts.) Add the egg yolk and stir vigorously. Pour the mixture into a shallow dish and jiggle to spread it into an even, smooth surface. Sprinkle with cinnamon and serve.

4. You can store leftovers in an airtight container, with a piece of plastic wrap in direct contact with the pudding, in the refrigerator for up to 5 days. The pudding can be eaten cold, at room temperature, or, even better, warmed a bit in the microwave.

WHEN IN PORTUGAL:

For special occasions, we make this rice pudding a little fancier by moistening the rim of a shot glass, dipping it in cinnamon, and pressing it gently into the top of the pudding to make a simple pattern just after it's been poured in the serving dish.

Coconut Custard Tarts
QUEIJADAS DE COCO

Prep time: 15 minutes | **Cook time:** 30 minutes

*Large families were commonplace in the Portugal of my parents'
generation. My father was one of nine siblings, which made for many
great parties when I was growing up. It seemed that every weekend of
my childhood was spent attending birthday parties, baptisms, First
Communions, graduations, or holiday celebrations. Sometimes we even
got together for no reason. At every event, my godmother would make
these creamy, crustless little treats.* **MAKES 18 TARTS**

Cooking spray

2 large eggs

1¼ cups sugar

4 tablespoons
  margarine, melted

¾ cups all-purpose flour

1 (2-inch) lemon peel

2 cups whole milk

½ cup sweetened
  shredded coconut

1. Preheat the oven to 375°F. Spray 3 (12-cup) muffin tins with cooking spray.

2. In a large bowl, whisk together the eggs and sugar. Add the margarine slowly
    while whisking briskly. Add the flour and lemon peel, and whisk to combine.
    Slowly add the milk while whisking. Add the coconut and carefully mix into
    the batter.

3. Remove the lemon peel and discard. Fill each muffin cup three-quarters of the
    way with batter, stirring before each pour.

4. Bake for 30 to 40 minutes, or until golden brown. The coconut will rise to the top
    and turn golden brown.

5. Let tarts cool in the muffin tins before removing. Each tart will be puffy when
    you first take them out of the oven, but they will fall in the center as they cool.

6. Place each tart in a cupcake liner and place on a serving platter.

7. You can store leftovers in an airtight container in the refrigerator for up
    to 5 days.

HELPFUL HINT:
I like to use a glass measuring cup with a spout for easy pouring of this very liquidy batter.

Custard Tart Cups

PASTÉIS DE NATA

Prep time: 30 minutes | **Cook time:** 18 minutes

One of the most recognizably Portuguese desserts, Pastéis de Nata, is a common choice for holiday celebrations and parties. The crispy shell provides stability and a savory contrast to the soft, sweet filling. As the custard skin puffs up in the super-hot oven, the tops should be dotted with little burn spots. If you don't see these spots, you haven't baked the tarts correctly. **MAKES 18 TART CUPS**

¼ cup shortening

2 sheets frozen puff pastry, thawed and cut into 18 squares

⅓ cup heavy (whipping) cream

2 cups sugar, plus 2 teaspoons

4 tablespoons all-purpose flour

2¼ cups whole milk, divided

3 large eggs

7 large egg yolks

1 cinnamon stick

1 (2-inch) lemon peel

1. Preheat the oven to 475°F. Grease 3 (6-cup) muffin tins with shortening.

2. Press a square of puff pastry into each muffin cup, using your fingers to form a crust that covers the entire cup. Brush the rim of each crust with cream. Sprinkle the 2 teaspoons sugar across the moistened pastry. Place the muffin tins on a baking sheet and set aside.

3. In a small bowl, whisk together the flour and ½ cup milk until smooth. Set aside.

4. In a large bowl, whisk together the eggs and egg yolks and set aside.

5. In a 3-quart saucepan over medium heat, mix together the remaining 1¾ cups milk, cinnamon stick, and lemon peel. While constantly whisking, slowly add the milk and flour mixture. Bring the mixture to a boil and immediately remove from the heat.

6. In a separate 2-quart saucepan over medium heat, mix together the remaining 2 cups sugar and 1 cup water, bring to a boil, and boil for 3 minutes. Remove from the heat.

7. Place a fine-mesh sieve over a large bowl. While whisking constantly, add the sugar mixture to the milk mixture and stir until completely incorporated. Pour the mixture into the sieve and strain out any lumps. Remove the lemon peel and discard.

8. Using a ladle, pour 1 ladleful liquid into the egg yolks and whisk constantly. Add the remaining liquid and continue to whisk until fully combined. Transfer the mixture to a measuring cup with a spout.

9. Pour the liquid into each prepared pastry cup just over three-quarters full. Bake for 15 to 18 minutes, until the tarts puff up and develop black spots.

10. You can store leftovers in an airtight container in the refrigerator for up to 5 days. These tarts taste best at room temperature, but you can eat them cold as well.

WHEN IN PORTUGAL:
This little tart is so synonymous with Portuguese cuisine that you would be hard-pressed to find a town in the whole country that does not serve these up in a café paired with an espresso.

Popovers with Lemon Icing

CAVACAS

Prep time: 10 minutes | Cook time: 35 minutes

These pastries are light, airy, and crispy. The only sweetness comes from the lemony icing drizzled over the top. Enjoy the popovers with a hot cup of tea or coffee. **MAKES 18 POPOVERS**

FOR THE POPOVERS

Nonstick cooking spray with flour

6 large eggs, at room temperature

1 teaspoon fine sea salt

2 cups sifted all-purpose flour

4 tablespoons margarine, melted, or vegetable oil

FOR THE ICING

2 cups confectioners' sugar

Whole peel of 1 lemon

TO MAKE THE POPOVERS

1. Preheat the oven to 375°F. Spray 3 (6-cup) muffin tins with cooking spray with flour. If you don't have that kind of spray, grease the muffin tins and dust them with all-purpose flour.

2. In the bowl of an electric mixer, beat the eggs on medium speed until light and frothy, about 2 minutes. Add the salt and beat 1 minute.

3. Add the flour and beat for 2 minutes on the lowest speed. Slowly stream in the melted margarine. The dough will look a little gummy.

4. Using an ice cream scoop with a retractable handle, fill the muffin cups with the dough.

5. Bake for 35 minutes. Do not open the oven to check them. Let the popovers cool in the pan for 5 minutes before transferring them to a large plate.

TO MAKE THE ICING

1. Place the confectioners' sugar in a 4-cup measuring cup with a spout. Place the lemon rind in the sugar, and add ¼ cup water. Whisk until smooth, letting the lemon rind sit in the icing.

2. When you're ready to ice the popovers, remove the lemon rind from the icing and discard. Pour the icing over the popovers in a slow, thin stream, crisscrossing in a random pattern. Let the icing harden. Serve the popovers at room temperature.

3. You can store the leftovers in an airtight container at room temperature for up to 5 days.

Vavó's Sponge Cake
PÃO DE LO

Prep time: 25 minutes | **Cook time:** 45 minutes

My grandmother was not a big baker, but when she did bake, she always made this sponge cake. In fact, I think this cake is the only reason she even owned an electric mixer—I never saw her use it for anything else. Now every time I make this cake, it brings me right back to being with my Vavó and enjoying a cup of tea and this deliciously simple dessert. **SERVES 8 TO 10**

Shortening, for greasing

2 cups all-purpose flour

1 teaspoon baking powder

8 large eggs, separated

2 cups sugar

1. Preheat the oven to 350°F. Grease and flour an angel food cake pan.

2. Sift the flour and baking powder into a large bowl and set aside.

3. Place the egg whites in the bowl of an electric mixer and beat until stiff. Transfer to another bowl and set aside. Place the egg yolks and sugar in the bowl of the electric mixer and beat until creamy.

4. Fold the whites into the yolk mixture. Add the flour mixture and mix to combine, scraping the sides of the bowl.

5. Pour the batter into the prepared pan and bake for 35 to 45 minutes, or until a toothpick inserted into the cake comes out clean.

6. Let the cake cool in the pan on a wire rack for 30 minutes before transferring to a cake plate and cutting into slices.

7. You can store leftovers in an airtight container at room temperature for up to 5 days.

PAIR IT WITH:

This is a dry cake, which makes it pair very well with coffee or tea. It can also be used as a base for strawberry shortcake. Simply top each piece with sliced strawberries and dollops of whipped cream.

Biscuit Rings

BISCOITS

Prep time: 30 minutes | **Cook time:** 30 minutes

Enter any Portuguese bakery and you're sure to see bags full of these crispy cookies that are an excellent companion to a hot cup of tea. As a little girl, I helped my mom and grandmother roll the dough into perfect rings, and at Christmastime, we colored half the dough red or green and twisted it into candy canes or wreaths. **MAKES 18 BISCUITS**

---

5 cups unbleached flour
½ teaspoon baking soda
½ teaspoon baking powder
1 cup sugar

4 large eggs
2 tablespoons salted butter, melted and cooled

2 tablespoons unsalted butter, melted and cooled

1. Preheat the oven to 375°F. Line a baking sheet with parchment paper.

2. In a large bowl, whisk together the flour, baking soda, and baking powder, and set aside.

3. In another large bowl, mix together the sugar and eggs. Add the salted and unsalted butters and mix well.

4. Add the sugar mixture to the flour mixture, and mix together until it forms a stiff dough without any streaks of flour.

5. Roll 2 tablespoons of dough into a ½-inch-thick rope and shape it into a 3-inch circle. You can also shape the dough into a candy cane. Place it on the prepared sheet. Repeat with the rest of the dough, spacing each cookie about ½ inch apart.

6. Bake for 30 minutes. Transfer the cookies to a wire rack and cool completely.

HELPFUL HINT:

You can make this dough ahead of time, store it in an zip-top bag, and freeze. To use, thaw the dough in the refrigerator overnight, then let sit for 30 to 60 minutes at room temperature before shaping and baking. You can also shape the dough first and freeze your cookies on a baking sheet lined with parchment paper. Once frozen, place the cookies in a zip-top bag and store in the freezer. Thaw completely before baking.

Fried Cinnamon Sugar Toast
FATIAS DOURADAS

Prep time: 30 minutes | **Cook time:** 18 minutes

My Vavó Olinda used to call these "sopas fritas," which never made much sense to me because the words literally translate as "fried soup." Here, we beat eggs, add milk, and dunk day-old bread into the mixture, which is then fried. This technique is actually closer to French toast than "fried soup." Fried Cinnamon Sugar Toast is traditionally served on Fat Tuesday, although in my family, we eat it for breakfast, at parties, or just as a fun snack. **MAKES 18 SLICES**

---

1 cup sugar

3 tablespoons ground cinnamon

6 large eggs

2 tablespoons milk

½ cup vegetable oil

1 large loaf day-old Vienna bread (or crusty bread of your choosing), cut into 18 (1-inch-thick) slices

1. In a large shallow bowl, mix together the sugar and cinnamon and set aside. In a separate large shallow bowl, whisk together the eggs and milk.

2. In a large nonstick skillet, heat the vegetable oil over medium-high heat.

3. Dip 1 slice bread into the milk mixture, making sure to coat the bread completely. Hold it over the bowl to let any excess liquid drip off. Place the dipped bread in the skillet and fry until golden brown, 2 to 3 minutes per side. Immediately dredge the fried bread in the cinnamon-sugar mixture and transfer to a large plate. Repeat with the remaining bread slices. Serve hot.

HELPFUL HINT:

Fried bread is great hot or at room temperature but does not store well, so eat it right away.

Festive Lollipops
DOCE DE FESTA

Prep time: 5 minutes | **Cook time:** 15 minutes

My daughter is always up for a cooking project, so when she heard my parents talking about the lollipops they would get at the feasts in their villages, we got to work. These pops are usually a light pastel color and shaped as animals. If you get really good at this recipe, you may want to try your hand at making shapes, but I usually just use sprinkles to give them a festive touch. **MAKES 12 LOLLIPOPS**

Shortening, for greasing

2 cups sugar

¾ cup light corn syrup

½ teaspoon candy flavoring (optional)

1 drop food coloring (optional)

1 teaspoon colorful candy sprinkles (optional)

1. In a bowl big enough to fit the saucepan you plan to use, mix together ice and cold tap water. Line a baking sheet with parchment paper greased with a very thin layer of shortening or with a silicone baking mat. Set aside.

2. Place a candy thermometer in a small heavy-bottomed stainless-steel saucepan over medium heat. Add the sugar, corn syrup, and ¼ cup water and stir once. Bring to a boil, taking care not to stir. Use a dampened silicone pastry brush to brush down the sides of the pan if any crystals form.

3. Continue to boil until the mixture reaches the hard crack stage of 305°F. Add the flavoring and food color, if using, and gently swirl the pan until the coloring is mixed in, not more than 15 seconds. Immediately remove from the heat and carefully place the pan in the ice water bath to stop the cooking process. Let sit for about 1 minute.

4. Carefully spoon about 1 tablespoon liquid onto the prepared sheet and place a lollipop stick in the liquid, rolling the stick a little to coat it with the liquid all the way around. Quickly add sprinkles, if using. Let cool in a cool, dry place (not the refrigerator) for 1 to 1½ hours, until completely hardened. Serve immediately.

5. You can store the lollipops, wrapped individually in plastic, at room temperature for up to 6 months.

HELPFUL HINT:
If you don't have flavoring, the plain pops are still delicious, but you can also boil the water with orange or lemon rinds, mint, or cinnamon sticks and cool it before adding to the sugar.

Meringues

SUSPIROS

Prep time: 30 minutes | **Cook time:** 45 minutes

As a little girl, I was amazed to see these meringues coming out of my Vavó Silva's oven. They seemed too perfect and too delicate for a real person to make. As my culinary skills improved, I realized that if I had an electric mixer, eggs, and sugar, I could easily make them myself. Melting the sugar before baking is a technique you won't find in many recipes, but I assure you, it's worth the extra five minutes. **MAKES 18 MERINGUES**

---

4 large egg whites
1½ cups sugar

1. Preheat oven to 225°F. Line a baking sheet with parchment paper.

2. Bring a large saucepan, with about 2 inches of water, to a simmer.

3. In the bowl of an electric mixer, beat the egg whites and sugar by hand for about 30 seconds.

4. Place the bowl over the saucepan of simmering water, and beat the egg mixture continuously until the sugar crystals have dissolved, 3 to 4 minutes. (This is an important step. Beating continuously builds volume and keeps the mixture moving so the eggs don't cook.)

5. With the electric mixer fitted with the whisk attachment, whisk the mixture for 4 to 5 minutes, until stiff peaks form.

6. Transfer the mixture to a piping bag or gallon-size freezer bag, fitted with a star tip or with the end cut off. Pipe the mixture in 3-inch circles on the prepared sheet.

7. Bake for 45 minutes without opening the oven. Turn off the oven and let the meringues cool completely in the oven.

8. You can store leftovers in an airtight container at room temperature for up to 2 weeks.

CHAPTER EIGHT

Drinks

Wine is king in Portugal. Just about every family can point to a homemade winemaker in their clan, and a huge percentage of the country is covered in vineyards. Now the liquor industry is making some waves of its own, with Portuguese gin distilleries attracting attention on the world stage and liqueurs of every variety finding their way into mixed drinks in the trendiest bars and night spots. The recipes here reflect all these Portuguese specialties.

Cherry Anisette Cocktail (page 108)

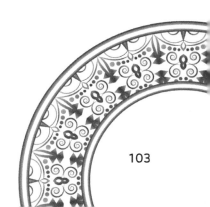

Red Sangria
SANGRIA VINHO TINTO

Prep time: 10 minutes

Red Sangria is a staple of Portuguese bars, restaurants, and family tables. This refreshing cocktail is a perfect accompaniment to grilled food and a great drink to make ahead for a party. **SERVES 6**

6 ounces orange juice

1 ounce triple sec

1 ounce brandy

750 milliliters red table wine

1 apple, sliced

1 orange, sliced, divided

1½ cups lemon-lime soda

2 cups ice

1. In a large pitcher, mix together the orange juice, triple sec, and brandy. Add the wine, apple slices, and half the orange slices and stir. Refrigerate for at least 6 hours and up to 24 hours.

2. When ready to serve, stir in the soda and ice. Garnish with the remaining orange slices.

White Peach Sangria
SANGRIA DE PÊSSEGO BRANCO

Prep time: 15 minutes

This summery Sangria is festive and elegant with slices of white peaches. If peaches aren't your thing, try mango or melon. **SERVES 6**

750 milliliters Vinho Verde

1 cup peach nectar

3 medium ripe white peaches, sliced

½ cup peach brandy

½ cup white rum

2 cups ice cubes

1 liter peach-flavored sparkling water or plain sparkling water

1. In a large pitcher, mix together the Vinho Verde, peach nectar, peaches, brandy, and rum. Refrigerate for at least 6 hours and up to 24 hours.

2. When ready to serve, add the ice and sparkling water. Serve immediately, making sure each glass gets a good amount of ice.

HELPFUL HINT:

Peach nectar is widely available at most grocers, but if you can't find it, just make your own. Dice three peaches and puree them in a blender until smooth. Place a kitchen towel over a large bowl. Transfer the puree to the kitchen towel and squeeze as much liquid into the bowl as possible. Discard the pulp. If the peaches are not very sweet, mix a few tablespoons sugar into the juice.

Wine Cooler

Prep time: 5 minutes

The rules of serving alcohol to minors are much more relaxed in Portuguese culture than in American culture. As children, my Vavó Olinda would often mix together water or lemon-lime soda, a good amount of sugar, and a splash of red wine and give it to us to drink if there wasn't anything else in the house. This recipe is a homage to my Vavó Olinda and all the other Portuguese grandmothers who did the same thing. **SERVES 2**

½ cup ice

1 cup lime-flavored
   sparkling water

½ cup sweet red table wine

2 tablespoons simple syrup
   or 2 heaping teaspoons
   white sugar

2 lime wedges

1. Place the ice in two large glasses. Pour half of the sparkling water, red wine, and simple syrup into each glass and stir.

2. Garnish with a lime wedge and serve immediately.

White Port and Tonic

PORTO TONICO

Prep time: 5 minutes

Port is a major part of the Portuguese drinking culture and is savored as an after-dinner drink. A less-celebrated version is white port, and although equally as sweet and made in the same region of Porto, it's considered fair game for mixing. **SERVES 2**

---

4 sprigs fresh
  lavender, divided

4 lemon slices, divided
1½ cups ice cubes

1 cup white port
2 cups tonic water

1. Place one sprig lavender and one lemon slice in each of two glasses.

2. Divide the ice cubes between the two glasses. Pour ½ cup white port over the ice in each glass, top with tonic water, and stir.

3. Garnish with the remaining lemon slices and lavender sprigs.

EASY SUBSTITUTION:

If you don't have fresh lavender available to you, try sprigs of fresh rosemary or mint. Just as delicious, I promise you.

Cherry Anisette Cocktail

ANISE DE CEREJAS

Prep time: 5 minutes

Portuguese home bars typically have some type of anise liqueur. This licorice-flavored spirit with a thread of crystallized sugar is often enjoyed as a single-ounce shot. But I love the combination of licorice and cherries, so I've created this sophisticated drink, which should impress the cocktail aficionado in your life. **SERVES 2**

½ cup coarse white sugar

Grated zest of 1 lime

3 lime wedges, divided

1 cup ice

2 ounces gin

2 ounces Portuguese
　anise liqueur

½ cup cherry juice

2 sour cherries or
　maraschino cherries

2 white rock-candy lollipops

1. Mix together the sugar and lime zest on a small plate. Use one lime wedge to moisten the rims of two martini glasses. Gently roll the moistened rim in the sugar and set aside.

2. In a cocktail shaker, add the lime wedge you used to rim the glasses, the ice, gin, anise liqueur, and cherry juice. Cover and shake vigorously. Strain into the prepared glasses.

3. Garnish each glass with a cherry and a rock-candy lollipop, and serve.

WHEN IN PORTUGAL:

Gin distilled in Portugal is just starting to make waves on the global market, so be on the lookout for more cocktails from these up-and-coming distilleries.

Stacy's Tropical Poncha

Prep time: 10 minutes

One of the most popular party drinks on the sunny island of Madeira features cachaça, the area's signature rum made from sugarcane. I've elevated the drink by adding freshly squeezed fruit juices and honey. I've specified locally sourced honey because the flavor is rich, but use any honey you like. **SERVES 2**

½ cup turbinado sugar or raw sugar

1 lemon, zested and cut into quarters

¼ cup cachaça (Madeiran rum), or other rum made from sugarcane

Juice of ½ lemon

2 tablespoons pineapple juice

2 tablespoons locally sourced honey

6 (1-inch) chunks fresh pineapple

Ice cubes

Juice of ½ orange

1. Mix together the turbinado sugar and lemon zest on a small plate. Moisten the rims of two glasses with one of the lemon wedges, dip the rims of the glasses into the mixture, and set aside.

2. In a large glass, mix together the cachaça, lemon juice, pineapple juice, and honey with a fork or a small whisk until the honey is dissolved.

3. Place the pineapple chunks and a few cubes of ice into each prepared glass. Pour the rum mixture over the ice, add a splash orange juice, and serve.

WHEN IN PORTUGAL:

There are many variations of this cocktail. For a more traditional version, eliminate the sugared rim and the pineapple. In Madeira, there is a hand-carved, long-handled wooden tool that is used just to stir this specific drink.

Caipirão

Prep time: 15 minutes

This drink is one of the hottest in Lisbon today. It's not very sweet, although Licor Beirão does have a sweetness to it. At most bars, it is made to order. Each element of the drink must be prepared in the order listed here to achieve an authentic Lisbon tavern taste. **SERVES 4**

---

1 large lime, diced

3 cups crushed ice

¾ cup Licor Beirão

4 lime slices, for garnish

1. Chill four heavy glasses.

2. Divide the lime between the four glasses, and use a cocktail muddler or the back of a wooden spoon to crush the limes in the bottom of each glass.

3. Divide the ice between the glasses. Pour 3 tablespoons Licor Beirão into each glass and stir.

4. Garnish with lime slices and serve immediately.

EASY SUBSTITUTION:

If you're looking for something on the sweeter side, swap out the limes here for passion fruit, a very popular fruit in Portugal.

Shaken Strawberry
MORANGÃO

Prep time: 2 minutes

This drink is best in late spring, when strawberries are at their peak. It can be served two ways. If you're after a more sophisticated drink, leave the ice and strawberries in the shaker. If you're looking for something a bit more fun, skip the shaking, add 2 more teaspoons of sugar, and put it all in a blender for a frozen delight. **SERVES 2**

5 fresh strawberries
½ teaspoon sugar

1 cup crushed ice
Juice of 1 lemon

2 ounces Licor Beirão
2 lime slices, for garnish

1. Chill two glasses.
2. Muddle the strawberries and sugar in the bottom of a cocktail shaker using a wooden spoon. Let sit for 1 minute to let the sugar melt a bit.
3. Add the ice, lemon juice, and Licor Beirão, cover, and shake for 15 seconds, until the sugar dissolves.
4. Pour into the chilled glasses and garnish with the lime slices.

EASY SUBSTITUTION:

If you use frozen strawberries or another type of berry, this drink will be just as delicious, but adjust the sugar to accommodate the sweetness of the berry you're using. For example, use a bit more sugar for blackberries and a bit less for sweet, ripe blueberries.

Queimada

Prep time: 2 minutes | Cook time: 10 minutes

If you're searching for a showstopper, look no further. This recipe involves open flames, so it's best made outside with spectators at a safe distance. Enjoy this drink with some bread and cheese to offset its sweetness or pair it with a warm plate of Rice Pudding (page 90). **SERVES 8**

---

1 liter aguardiente or grappa

¾ cup sugar

1 large piece of lemon or lime peel

¼ cup coffee beans

1 cinnamon stick

1. Place a clay pot or stone bowl capable of sustaining high heat in a safe place, such as an outdoor marble surface or grilling area. Be sure to have a large lid beside the pot for extinguishing the flames.

2. Fill the pot with the aguardiente and sugar, and stir until the sugar is completely dissolved. Add the lemon or lime peel, coffee beans, and cinnamon stick.

3. Using a long-necked lighter, such as used to light a grill, carefully light the liquid. Let the flames burn until the liquid is hot, stirring occasionally with a long-handled metal spoon, 8 to 10 minutes. Use the lid to extinguish the flames.

4. Ladle into coffee mugs and serve hot.

CHAPTER NINE

Marinades, Sauces, and Staples

Spices are the backbone of Portuguese cuisine. Portuguese explorers collected spices from all over the world, and the influence of their journeys is strongly reflected in this chapter's marinades, sauces, and breads.

Bread Rolls (page 127)

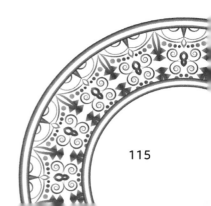

Chouriço Marinade
MOLHO DE CHOURIÇO

Prep time: 10 **minutes, plus** 12 **hours to rest**

This marinade uses the same flavors in chouriço. If you have a chance to visit a meat market that specializes in producing chouriço, you'll likely find both this marinade and cuts of pork tenderloin soaked in the marinade. Whatever meat you use, be sure to let it marinate for at least 1 hour (and ideally much longer). **MAKES ABOUT 2 CUPS**

1 cup warm water
½ cup dry white wine
½ cup sweet paprika
¼ cup smoked paprika
¼ cup red wine vinegar

2 tablespoons coarse
   kosher salt
1 tablespoon
   granulated garlic
1 tablespoon olive oil

1 teaspoon Pimenta
   Moida (page 121) or red
   pepper flakes
½ teaspoon freshly ground
   white pepper
1 dried bay leaf

1. In a container with a lid, whisk together the warm water, wine, sweet paprika, smoked paprika, vinegar, salt, granulated garlic, olive oil, Pimenta Moida, and white pepper until if forms a thin paste. Add the bay leaf and continue whisking until the salt has dissolved.

2. Cover and refrigerate overnight before using. You can store in the refrigerator for up to 1 week.

Basic Meat Marinade

VINHA D'ALHO

Prep time: 10 minutes

This easy marinade recipe is sufficient for about three pounds of meat. Make a batch and use it right away, or double the recipe and freeze half for later use. You can also freeze your meat in this marinade. The meat marinates while it's defrosting. **MAKES ABOUT 2½ CUPS**

---

1 medium onion, cut into small dice

6 to 8 garlic cloves, crushed

2 cups dry white wine or beer

2 dried bay leaves

2 tablespoons Pimenta Moida (page 121)

2 teaspoons freshly squeezed lemon juice

½ teaspoon Portuguese All Spice (page 123)

2 tablespoons red wine vinegar

½ teaspoon freshly ground white pepper

1 tablespoon coarse kosher salt or sea salt

1. In a large bowl, combine all the ingredients.

2. The marinade alone can be stored in an airtight container and refrigerated for up to 1 week or frozen for up to 6 months. You can also store the meat and marinade together in the refrigerator for 48 hours or in the freezer for 3 months.

HELPFUL HINT:

If you're planning to marinate something overnight, do not add the lemon until 2 hours before cooking.

Fish Sauce

MOLHO DE VILÃO

Prep time: 10 minutes | **Cook time:** 25 minutes

You'll rarely find fish on a Portuguese menu without some kind of sauce. This sauce elevates fried, poached, or baked fish. Make more than you need and freeze the rest so you have it on hand, and don't be afraid to try it on pork or chicken. **MAKES ABOUT 1 CUP**

¼ cup olive oil

8 garlic cloves, sliced

1 large hot chile pepper, seeded and chopped

¼ cup white vinegar

1 tablespoon minced fresh flat-leaf parsley

½ teaspoon coarse kosher salt

¼ teaspoon freshly ground white pepper

1. In a small skillet, heat the olive oil over medium-low heat. Add the garlic and cook, stirring constantly, for 2 minutes. Add the hot chile pepper and sauté until tender. Raise the heat to medium-high, add the vinegar, and bring to a boil.

2. Remove from the heat and stir in the parsley, salt, and white pepper.

HELPFUL HINT:

If you favor heat, keep the seeds when you chop up the chile pepper. I often wear disposable latex gloves when I'm working with hot chiles.

Vinegar Sauce

MOLHO CRU

Prep time: 10 minutes | **Cook time:** 24 hours to rest

In Portugal, which has strong Catholic roots, Friday is fish day. In my family, this tradition involves fish with this vinegar-based sauce.

MAKES ABOUT 1¼ CUPS

---

1 large shallot, diced

1 cup red wine vinegar

1 teaspoon Pimenta Moida (page 121) or ½ hot chile, seeded and finely diced

1 teaspoon minced fresh flat-leaf parsley

1. In a mason jar, add all the ingredients, cover with the lid, and shake to combine. Let sit for at least 24 hours and up to 48 hours. Serve over fried fish.

2. Store in the refrigerator for up to 2 months.

HELPFUL HINT:

This recipe is enough for about six people, but if you make fish and chips more than once a month, I suggest doubling or tripling and keeping it on hand in the refrigerator for up to 2 months.

Pepper Sauce

MOLHO DE PIMENTA

Prep time: 10 minutes | Cook time: 15 minutes

This sauce is perfect for fish, pork, and fried chicken, but I also love it over boiled thin-skinned potatoes. Try it in recipes like Pepper-Stuffed Potatoes (page 21). **MAKES ABOUT ½ CUP**

2 tablespoons olive oil
½ small onion, minced
4 garlic cloves, minced or put through a garlic press

4 tablespoons Pimenta Moida (page 121)
¼ teaspoon Portuguese All Spice (page 123)

1 teaspoon minced fresh flat-leaf parsley
Kosher salt

1. In a small skillet, heat the olive oil over medium-low heat. Add the onion and cook until translucent, 5 to 6 minutes. Add the garlic and cook for 2 minutes. Add the Pimenta Moida and All Spice and cook for 5 minutes.

2. Remove from the heat and add the parsley and salt. Use warm or at room temperature.

EASY SUBSTITUTION:

If you don't have Pimenta Moida, grind a seeded red chile pepper (like an Anaheim chile), add it with the All Spice, and cook an additional 5 minutes.

Pimenta Moida

Prep time: 1 hour | **Cook time:** 48 to 72 hours to ferment,
plus 72 hours to rest

*My Vavô Fernando always said the best peppers were found at the farmers'
market on the day after a full moon. He believed those peppers had less
liquid. My dad has always been the assigned pepper-grinding person in our
family, and he doesn't use gloves because his hands have become immune to
the capsaicin. I made the mistake of not wearing gloves and my hands were
red and burning for two days!* **MAKES 2 TO 3 CUPS**

| 2 dozen hot red peppers | ½ cup kosher salt, plus more for topping | 2 tablespoons preserving powder, like ascorbic acid |

1. While wearing latex or rubber gloves, wash and dry the peppers.

2. Cut the peppers in half lengthwise, and remove the stems and seeds.

3. Using an old-fashioned grinder or the grinder attachment on your stand mixer, grind the peppers into a large stainless-steel bowl.

4. Add the salt and stir to combine. Cover the bowl with a clean dish cloth.

5. Let the bowl sit at room temperature for 24 to 72 hours. The peppers will ferment or boil, a process that uses the heat from the capsaicin in the pepper itself.

6. When you observe a reduction in the boiling, add the preserving powder and stir to combine.

7. Let the mixture sit at room temperature, covered, for an additional 24 hours.

8. Stir again and transfer the mixture to sanitized containers like canning jars. Place the lids on loosely. Let sit for an additional 72 hours.

9. Tighten the lids and store the containers at room temperature.

10. Once a jar is opened, store it in the refrigerator for up to 8 months.

HELPFUL HINT:

My family's recipe is quite mild, but if you prefer something a little more spicy, leave a few seeds in the mix.

Onion Medley
CEBOLADA

Prep time: 10 minutes | **Cook time:** 35 to 40 minutes

There are two main ways to prepare Cebolada: plain or with tomato. This recipe is plain and goes with any number of codfish dishes. Tomatoes are added in the recipe for Taro Root with Onion Medley (page 33). To make the medley with tomato, put two diced tomatoes in the skillet after you add the onion. **MAKES ABOUT 2 CUPS**

¼ cup olive oil, plus more for drizzling

2 large yellow onions, cut into thin rings

Kosher salt

2 garlic cloves, crushed

1 teaspoon Pimenta Moida (page 121)

¼ teaspoon freshly ground white pepper

⅛ teaspoon Portuguese All Spice (page 123) or paprika

1. In a large skillet, heat the olive oil over medium heat. Add the onions and cook for 5 minutes. Lower the heat, add a pinch salt, and continue to cook, stirring frequently, for 20 minutes.

2. Add the garlic and cook for another 2 minutes. Add the peppers and All Spice and cook for 6 to 8 minutes.

3. Drizzle with olive oil. Add salt to taste. Serve warm or at room temperature.

Portuguese All Spice

TEMPEROS PORTUGUESES

Prep time: 10 minutes | **Cook time:** 25 minutes

If you live in southeastern New England, you'll be able to find this spice mixture at any Portuguese market. I thought it was sold everywhere, but when I started blogging, I found out All Spice is not easily available. To fill the gap, I came up with my own version. Note that Portuguese All Spice is nothing like allspice, which is not a blend. **MAKES ABOUT ½ CUP**

Grated zest of 1 orange

4 tablespoons
  sweet paprika

1 tablespoon
  granulated garlic

1 teaspoon ground turmeric

1 teaspoon onion powder

½ teaspoon freshly ground
  white pepper

1. Preheat the oven to 275°F. Line a baking sheet with parchment paper.

2. Place the zest on the prepared sheet and bake for 25 minutes, or until the zest is dried. Let cool completely. Using a spice grinder, grind the zest into a powder.

3. In a small mason jar or an airtight container, add all the ingredients, cover with a lid, and shake to mix thoroughly.

4. You can store the spice mixture in a sealed jar at room temperature for up to 1 year.

HELPFUL HINT:

Add ½ teaspoon spice mixture to onion and garlic that have been sautéed in olive oil, and you are well on your way to infusing Portuguese flavors to almost any protein. Just be careful not to overdo it; you don't want to overpower the dish's flavor.

Corn Bread

PÃO DE MILO

Prep time: 3 hours, including rest time | Cook time: 45 minutes

Corn bread was usually served in Portuguese households because wheat flour was too expensive for most families to use on a regular basis. In more traditional recipes, only corn flour would be used, but here I have combined it with all-purpose flour to make the bread a bit less dense. It's also common not to add sugar, as is typical in American corn bread recipes.

MAKES 2 TO 3 MEDIUM LOAVES

FOR THE SPONGE

2½ teaspoons active dry yeast

½ cup warm water (about 110°F)

1 tablespoon unbleached all-purpose flour

FOR THE DOUGH

6 to 6½ cups boiling water, divided

2 tablespoons kosher salt

2 pounds white corn flour (yellow can be used in a pinch, but not cornstarch or cornmeal)

2 pounds unbleached all-purpose flour, plus more for dusting

TO MAKE THE SPONGE

Mix together yeast, water, and flour in a medium bowl and set aside for at least 15 minutes. When bubbly and growing, it's ready for use.

TO MAKE THE DOUGH

1. In a medium bowl, mix together the water and salt until dissolved. Set aside.

2. In the bowl of an electric mixer, add the corn flour. With the mixer on low, add 6 cups salted water and mix until incorporated. The dough will be lumpy. Set aside and let cool for 10 minutes.

3. Switch to the dough hook on the electric mixer. Add the flour to the corn flour mixture and mix to combine. Add the yeast and mix. (It's important to follow this order, as the all-purpose flour helps cool the mixture, ensuring the yeast is not killed when added.) If the dough looks dry, add in the remaining ½ cup salted water a little at a time until the dough comes together. Knead in the mixer for about 10 minutes.

4. Remove the dough from the bowl, divide it into 2 or 3 pieces, and form them into balls. Dust each ball heavily with all-purpose flour and place each in a bowl. Cover with clean kitchen towels and let rise until doubled, 2 to 3 hours.

5. Preheat the oven to 475°F with a pizza stone set inside (you can also use a flour-dusted baking or cast-iron skillet). Gently remove the dough balls from the bowls and place them directly on the hot stone. Bake for 40 to 45 minutes, until browned. Let cool on a wire rack or in a large open paper bag.

HELPFUL HINT:
The interior of the bread will be somewhat moist and tender. For a bread that is drier, like traditional corn bread, bake for 15 minutes, then reduce the temperature to 375°F for the rest of the baking time.

Seared Corn Bread

BOLO DE SERTÃO

Prep time: 10 minutes | **Cook time:** 20 minutes

My mother shared her memories of my Vavó making Bolo de Sertão, usually to go along with the fish. She put a little flour in a flat clay pan, cooked the bread slowly, and wrapped it in a kitchen towel to keep it warm. Crunchy on the outside and almost creamy inside, its simple flavor makes it the perfect complement to flavorful fried fish. **SERVES 4**

2 cups corn flour, plus more for frying

1½ teaspoons fine sea salt

1 to 1½ cups boiling water

1. In a large bowl, sift together the corn flour and salt.

2. Form a well in the center of the corn flour. Add 1 cup boiling water and let it sit for a minute. Using a spoon, stir the mixture together. When cool enough to touch, knead the dough with your hands until it comes together like clay. (If the mixture is too dry, add boiling water, 1 teaspoon at a time; if the mixture is too loose, add corn flour, 1 teaspoon at a time.)

3. Place a heavy-bottomed skillet over medium-low heat and dust with flour. Form the dough into a disk and place it in the skillet. Cook until lightly browned on the bottom, about 10 minutes. Flip and cook until the other side is browned, about 5 minutes.

4. Cut into 8 pieces and serve with your favorite fried fish.

Bread Rolls

PAPO-SECOS

Prep time: 20 minutes, plus 8 hours to rest | Cook time: 15 to 20 minutes

Modern-day Portuguese meals are not complete without rolls and butter on the table. Breakfast might consist of Papo-secos and some butter and cheese, with tea or coffee. Crusty on the outside and soft on the inside, these rolls can be cut in half and made into sandwiches. My father uses them as hamburger rolls. Be sure to use wheat gluten to achieve bakery-level rolls. Papo-secos are best eaten the day they're baked. **MAKES 12 ROLLS**

FOR THE SPONGE

1¼ teaspoons active
   dry yeast
½ cup warm distilled
   water (100°F)
½ cup bread flour

FOR THE DOUGH

3 cups bread flour
1 tablespoon vital wheat
   gluten (optional)
1 tablespoon shortening
1 tablespoon fine sea salt

1¼ teaspoons active
   dry yeast
2 teaspoons sugar
1 to 1¼ cups warm
   water, divided
2 tablespoons rice flour

TO MAKE THE SPONGE

Stir the yeast, water, and flour together, and cover. Set aside and allow to develop overnight (at least 8 hours).

TO MAKE THE DOUGH

1. In the bowl of an electric mixer, add the flour and vital wheat gluten (if using), and stir to combine. Add the shortening and, using clean hands, pinch the shortening into the flour.

2. With the paddle attachment in place, add the salt, yeast, and sugar, and mix for 1 minute.

3. With the dough hook attachment, add the prepared sponge and 1 cup warm water, and mix until the dough comes together. If the dough seems dry, add the remaining ¼ cup warm water and mix on high speed for about 15 minutes to allow the gluten to develop. The dough should be stiff and elastic.

CONTINUED

4. Place the dough in a clear floured bowl, cover with a clean kitchen towel, and set aside to rise in a warm spot until doubled in size, about 2 hours. Punch down the dough and cover again. Let the dough rise again for about 1 hour.

5. When dough has risen again, punch down again, and roll the dough into a log. Cut the dough into 12 equal pieces and let rest for about 30 minutes.

6. Dust 2 baking sheets with rice flour.

7. Flatten each piece of dough into a disk. Tightly roll the left and right sides of the dough into the middle until they meet to make a roll. Place 6 dough rolls on each prepared sheet. Cover with a kitchen towel and set aside to rise again for about 1 hour.

8. Place a 9-by-13-inch metal baking pan filled with water on the bottom rack and a pizza stone on the center rack of the oven. Preheat the oven to 400°F for 30 minutes. Place the rolls on the heated stone and bake for 15 to 20 minutes until a light golden–brown color.

9. Let cool to the touch before serving.

HELPFUL HINT:
If you're not planning to eat this bread within 24 hours of baking, place the rolls in a zip-top bag and freeze for up to 6 weeks. To reheat, warm on a baking sheet in a 350°F oven for 10 minutes, or until warmed through.

Rustic Bread

PÃO CASEIRO

Prep time: 2 hours, including rest time | **Cook time:** 30 to 40 minutes

This easy bread recipe is a great introduction to the world of bread baking. You can make it the easy way with an electric mixer, as the recipe indicates, or by hand with an extra ten minutes of elbow grease. Fruit juice provides acid and a sweet note. **MAKES 1 LARGE LOAF OR 2 SMALL LOAVES**

---

1 cup warm water

1 teaspoon kosher salt

4 cups all-purpose flour

2½ teaspoons active
  dry yeast

1 teaspoon sugar

⅓ cup orange juice
  or unsweetened
  pineapple juice

⅓ cup light cream or
  whole milk

2 tablespoons olive
  oil, divided

1 teaspoon coarse cornmeal,
  for dusting

1 large egg yolk

1 tablespoon cool water

1. In a small bowl, mix together the warm water and salt until it dissolves. Set aside.

2. In the bowl of an electric mixer fitted with the dough hook, add the flour, yeast, sugar, orange juice, and cream, and mix together. Add the salted water and continue to mix for about 1 minute. Add 1 tablespoon olive oil and mix to combine.

3. When the dough forms a ball, remove it from the bowl and knead it for one minute by hand to ensure that it has been completely incorporated.

4. Pour the remaining 1 tablespoon olive oil into the used mixing bowl. Place the dough back into the bowl and turn the dough to coat it with the oil. Sprinkle the top of the dough with additional flour, cover with a clean kitchen towel, and let rise until doubled in size, about 1 hour.

5. Remove from the bowl and knead by hand for about 1 minute.

6. Preheat the oven to 400°F. Line a pizza stone or baking sheet with parchment paper and dust with cornmeal.

7. Form the dough into a ball and place on the prepared stone. Cover with a kitchen towel and let rise again for about 15 to 20 minutes.

CONTINUED

8. In a small bowl, beat together the egg and cool water to make an egg wash. Brush the egg wash over the dough and cut a slit into the top with a sharp knife.

9. Bake for 30 to 40 minutes, or until a dark golden brown. Cool on a wire rack or in a large open paper bag.

PAIR IT WITH:

This bread is wonderful sliced and spread with real cream salted butter or with a quick dip made with olive oil, salt, red pepper flakes, and grated Parmesan cheese.

Measurement Conversions

	U.S. Standard	U.S. Standard (ounces)	Metric (approximate)
VOLUME EQUIVALENTS (LIQUID)	2 tablespoons	1 fl. oz.	30 mL
	¼ cup	2 fl. oz.	60 mL
	½ cup	4 fl. oz.	120 mL
	1 cup	8 fl. oz.	240 mL
	1½ cups	12 fl. oz.	355 mL
	2 cups or 1 pint	16 fl. oz.	475 mL
	4 cups or 1 quart	32 fl. oz.	1 L
	1 gallon	128 fl. oz.	4 L
VOLUME EQUIVALENTS (DRY)	⅛ teaspoon	———	0.5 mL
	¼ teaspoon	———	1 mL
	½ teaspoon	———	2 mL
	¾ teaspoon	———	4 mL
	1 teaspoon	———	5 mL
	1 tablespoon	———	15 mL
	¼ cup	———	59 mL
	⅓ cup	———	79 mL
	½ cup	———	118 mL
	⅔ cup	———	156 mL
	¾ cup	———	177 mL
	1 cup	———	235 mL
	2 cups or 1 pint	———	475 mL
	3 cups	———	700 mL
	4 cups or 1 quart	———	1 L
	½ gallon	———	2 L
	1 gallon	———	4 L
WEIGHT EQUIVALENTS	½ ounce	———	15 g
	1 ounce	———	30 g
	2 ounces	———	60 g
	4 ounces	———	115 g
	8 ounces	———	225 g
	12 ounces	———	340 g
	16 ounces or 1 pound	———	455 g

	Fahrenheit (F)	Celsius (C) (Aproximate)
OVEN TEMPERATURES	250°F	120°C
	300°F	150°C
	325°F	180°C
	375°F	190°C
	400°F	200°C
	425°F	220°C
	450°F	230°C

Resources

For the best Portuguese chouriço and linguica, I buy from Michael's Provisions in Fall River, Massachusetts. The sausages are offered whole or ground by the pound, and the links are sold in hot and mild varieties. They ship throughout the United States (508-672-0982; michaelsprovision.com).

For Portuguese goods shipped throughout the United States:

Portugalia Marketplace in Fall River: For codfish, olive oils, sausage, and dry goods (508-617-9820; portugaliamarketplace.com).

Chaves Market in Fall River: For sausage, baked goods, olive oils, dry goods, and Portuguese imports (508-672-7821; chavesmarket.com).

For an online only retailer, check out PortugueseFood.com, which ships cheeses, sausage, pottery, and Portuguese paraphernalia (portuguesefood.com).

For Portuguese food shipped throughout Canada fermafoods.com.

Index

Acknowledgments

My mother, Natalia, will be the first to tell you: She is not someone who has a love of cooking. That said, she's a good Portuguese cook when she wants to be. My love of cooking really started when she began teaching me (while also allowing me to have independence in the kitchen from a very young age). Sure, I was influenced a lot by watching my dad, Tony, and my Vavô Fernando tend freshly grown ingredients in our garden; by enjoying meals around my Vavó Olinda's table; and by attending family parties each weekend where my aunts would bring mouthwatering dishes to share. But it all comes down to the sense of freedom that was all around me, which allowed me to create, fail, and move forward with never-ending encouragement. For that, I thank you, Mom and Dad.

About the Author

Stacy Silva-Boutwell lives in her hometown of Westport, Massachusetts, with her husband, Brian, and two children, Lucas and Alaina. She runs a cake design and event planning business and also manages her cooking and lifestyle blog, *The Portuguese American Mom* (thePAMom.com). Her community work includes teaching cooking classes for her local recreation department.

Stacy has been honored with professional accolades for her baked goods at the Battle of the Cupcakes and the Westport Fair. She has been featured for her culinary talents in publications such as *The Herald News*, *The Standard-Times*, *Taunton Daily Gazette*, and *South Coast Almanac*.

Stacy's parents moved from the Azores island of São Miguel to the United States in the 1960s. An active participant in the large Portuguese community around her, Stacy regularly attends Portuguese feasts and represents the community with pride through her culinary teachings and demonstrations.

CPSIA information can be obtained
at www.ICGtesting.com
Printed in the USA
JSHW031929070620
6120JS00004B/12

9 781646 116447